DEDICATION

❊ ❊ ❊ ❊

**To SCOTT ADAMS and DILBERT who have
encouraged us to laugh at ourselves and
have been a source of inspiration**

No-Bull Management

Printed in the United States of America

CONTENTS

Foreword by Joe Batten

Introduction   1

1. Clicking with Your Boss   13

2. Working with Turkeys   24

3. Surviving Leadership Training   33

4. Cultivating Your Image   43

5. Guarding Against Re-engineering
   (and Other Forms of Corporate Capital
   Punishment)   52

6. Coping with Political Correctness   61

7. Surviving Downsizing (and Your Next
   Reorganization)   73

8. Selling Your Ideas   81

9. Dealing with Bureaucrats   91

10. Honing Your Leadership Skills   100

11. Moving On   108

12. Lessons Learned   116

    Appendix—Challenges   120

    Final Exam

CRITICAL ACCLAIM
FOR *NO-BULL MANAGEMENT!*

"You can see how this book helped me."
—*Boris Yellstin*

"It works in practice—but will it work in theory?"
—*Harveid Business School*

"Biggest piece of trash ever published—but we liked it anyway."
—The Nationale Enquirer

"If only I had read this book I would still be the Prime Minister!"
—*K. T. Campbel, former Prime Minister of Canada with tenure of two months*

"This book describes the 'real world'—and is therefore inappropriate for business students or academicians."
—*The Northern School of Business*

"I have no interest in reading this book"
—*Head, Task Force on Improving Government Efficiency*

"Quite simply today's most important business book, and you can quote me on that."
—*Anonymous*

"I wish they had taught this at the University of Arkansas."
—*B. Clinton*

"This is required reading for all new interns."
Monica L.

"I wish I had passed this on to my two sons."
—*George Busch*

Foreword

Perusing *No-Bull Management* is a sheer delight! Having worked as a Management Consultant in organizations of all kinds all over the world, I found this tongue-in-cheek wisdom of Herb Gabora to be delicious.

Herb, a seasoned and brilliant management pro, takes deadly aim at the plethora of pliant platitudes and trite truisms which currently infest organizations of all kinds. This book is a blend of continuous chuckles saturated with practical truths and insights.

If you like *Dilbert*, you'll love Herb's *No-Bull Management*. Without any bull in your life, you will not suffer from excessive "Angus."

—JOE BATTEN, Author of *Tough-Minded Leadership, The Master Motivator*, and *The Leadership Principles of Jesus*

INTRODUCTION

We have now acquired the ability for computerized incompetence.

—B. Gates

Our challenge is to stop seizing defeat from the jaws of victory.

—Beth Dole

We have met the enemy, and he is us.   *—Pogo*

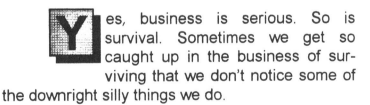**Y**es, business is serious. So is survival. Sometimes we get so caught up in the business of surviving that we don't notice some of the downright silly things we do.

Give Yourself the Bird's-eye View

Now and then back off from the arena, and observe that corporate life can devolve into the ludicrous. Many of the most memorable human interest stories develop in the workplace. The foibles, qualms, pleasures, puzzlements, and frustrations of today's work environments are the protoplasm of most Americans' everyday experiences. And what do most people gab about when they get together with fellow employees for happy hour or other "loosen-uppers" after working hours? Office politics.

Throw out clichés from past generations. Unless they have amazing communications skills with other generations, Generation X-ers are not even acquainted with a pop song older than five years. **But they know what bull means! And you most certainly do!**

The concept for *No-Bull Management* evolved over my lifetime of work as a senior executive, business consultant, and university instructor. I have tried to define and refine distinctions between managers who seemed successful and those who were, er, not as successful. As an exec at four well-known international companies, I was utterly intrigued at what certain managers pulled off and got away with . . . at least for the time being.

Theory vs. Practice

There is a glaring inconsistency between management theory in textbooks and actual business practice. My observations about this distinction surfaced as I published articles in scholarly journals while teaching at different business schools and conducting seminars in Canada, the United States, Europe, and Japan.

These ideas further developed while, as a consultant, I observed managers in action. So, in my examination of businesses I was fascinated by the charades, posturing and game-playing going on . . . all cleverly disguised as work, of course. These were not the practices described in management theory textbooks.

Times: They Are A'changin

And how! Our parents (if they were faithful to the firm, worked hard 40 dull hours a week, and avoided moral turpitude) could depend on remaining with the same company until voluntary retirement (which included the usual dinner party, toasts, a watch . . . and bad jokes).

The Chilling Winds of Uncertainty

Today harsh, gale-force winds of change are blowing across the landscape of America's corporate culture—in fact, throughout the world. One ill wind is the mounting obsession with work. The average North American works longer hours, and usually under more duress, than previously.

A second tornadic current is a growing fear in the workplace involving corporate changes that cause downsizing and restructuring. All of us have friends and relatives who have suffered the

3

ignominy of "being redundant."

The third gust is the festering irritation with seemingly endless management fads. As the lifespan of these voguish, but often unworkable, techniques becomes shorter, Ms. Average Jane and Mr. Average Joe grit their teeth and groan, "Good grief, here it comes again!" What was "in" yesterday is "out" today. And you have to make sure your vocabulary of buzz words is current.

What'll You Do? What Can You Do?

Joe South in the early 1970s sang, "Oh, the games people play now . . ." With these scary changes impacting the corporate environment, games people play at the office proliferate.

So what do you do? Do you play the games? Are you in the rat race? Are the rats winning?

So you want to get ahead? What are your options? That depends on your present situation. Pause at this juncture and fill out the *No-Bull Management Audit* to determine your baseline score. Now that you have determined where you are now, you can set goals for the future and contemplate the following possibilities for enhancing your career.

1. Keep Your Head Down In the Bunker

An ostrich-like approach is to avoid like the plague all interest in organizational politics. Press forward, glancing neither left nor right, keeping your bloody and bruised head down, chanting to yourself this mantra, "For the good of the company, for the good of the company, but I am not an unbiased, non-

NO-BULL MANAGEMENT AUDIT

1. When a co-worker pats you on the back, is there usually a knife involved?

1	2	3	4	5	6	7	8	9	10
occasionally				sometimes				frequently	

2. Problem-solving at work usually involves:

1	2	3	4	5	6	7	8	9	10
fixing the problem				hiding the evidence			passing the buck		

3. Meetings in our office usually provide an opportunity to:

1	2	3	4	5	6	7	8	9	10
make decisions				sleep in peace			off load decisions		

4. Project management around here means that:

1	2	3	4	5	6	7	8	9	10
It's in control.				All team members have updated their resumes.				It'll take a miracle.	

5. Communications around here usually provide a foundation for:

1	2	3	4	5	6	7	8	9	10
potential agreement				covering your area			total confusion		

6. Teamwork around here usully means that:

1	2	3	4	5	6	7	8	9	10
Everyone pulls in the same direction.				Most pull in the same direction.			Everyone pulls in different directions.		

7. My boss provides direction by:

1	2	3	4	5	6	7	8	9	10
documenting the rules				changing the rules at any time without prior notification			expecting me to mindread at all times		

SCORING: 0-20 Pass this book on to a friend.
30-50 Read it rwice.
60-70 Wear a flak jacket!

5

political animal in this morass of organizational brouhaha." (Most bank vice-presidents have managed to master this non-confrontational stance.)

You could convince yourself that it's magnifique down in the bunker—as you crouch frozen to the bone, fingers in your ears, trying to shut out the conflict being waged directly above your head. The stark reality is: strive to avoid the war however you can, but you cannot locate a lasting asylum from the skirmishes of organizational life. And like mud-slogging or sand-breathing foot soldiers (depending on the area of the conflict) in an ill-defined conflict, you're in infinitely more peril when you merely close your eyes and fervently hope.

2. Go To Business School

One of the most daunting issues for business today is the training and development of competent managers. Now, the administrators and faculties of business schools can place me on their dirty list . . . but business schools are too often notoriously ineffectual at preparing their students to accept the mantle of *leadership* required of effective managers.

Here are five valid reasons why it's better to read *No-Bull Management* than to attend a business school:

☺ There is no wasted travel time going to class (in fact, reading this guide in bed is recommended);

☺ There is no requirement for an interpreter (this guide is written in English rather than management jargon);

6

BEFORE reading this book.

AFTER reading this book.

☺ You will not encounter "the slings and arrows" of surly professors (or librarians);

☺ It's far less expensive (and if you are rather young, why launch into adult life saddled with a mega-thousand-dollar debt?);

☺ It includes only one exam (see last chapter).

3. Read and Apply No-Bull Management Survival Strategies

If you want to understand the intricate survival strategies of the corporate jungle, then *No-Bull Management* will demonstrate to you time-tested trails, then roads, and finally paved avenues to success.

This tome does not make a pretense of supplanting the efforts (however wrong-headed) of business schools. It does lay down a simple, easy-to-follow guide for the up-and-coming leader.

HOW TO USE THIS GUIDE

1. Executive Summary

To accommodate today's harassed executive, this indispensable manual has provided a concise, uncluttered summary of key points. Thus, you won't have to while away the hours actually reading the guide (and you can check it off on your list of consummately done self-development endeavors). This section is rendered in a style you are familiar with . . . a flow chart of main points (no emotions, for they tend to run amok). With BIG pictures and

These are not the
practices described in
management theory textbooks.

BIG type, it is perfect for executives who typically have short attention spans!

2. Leader's Survival Guide

This section provides a how-to kit for surviving in the corporate maze. It examines typical situations you will confront at work, describing what you should establish as your goal, then outlining the necessities for you to come out on top. (The situations described are totally factual, and any resemblance to reality is . . . strictly intentional.)

3. Academic Summary

If your field is academia, this packed section affords you an overview (and underview as well) of the chapter in a language (and its various shades of dialect) you may amazingly understand: i. e., incomparable baffle-gab. If you are a government bureaucrat, read this section three times, meld in recycled clichés in the margins, and then route it to your executive assistant for confirmation as to the fog index.

If you are in the legal field, avail yourself of this jargon at your discretion and make sure to add a hefty fee onto your client's invoice. If you are a consultant, it is of critical import for you to use these buzzwords, ensuring they are as incomprehensible as possible, thus establishing the undisputed verity that you are more intellectual than anyone and everyone else.

NOTE: Any relationship between the charts, graphs, and illustrations used in this guide and the lessons in the text are merely coincidental.

Illustrations are spread before you lest you do not have the time to read and absorb this guide.

EVERY RULE OF PUBLISHING
DECLARES THAT A LEFT-HAND
PAGE, ESPECIALLY BEFORE THE
FIRST CHAPTER, CAN BE BLANK
WITH NO NUMBER. OR, THIS
WOULD BE A PERFECT PAGE FOR
A LEFT-OUT CARTOON OR NEW
COPY. LET ME KNOW.

1. Clicking with Your Boss

My boss' style makes Attila the Hun look like a pacifist.

—Name Withheld by Request

There are an enormous number of managers who have retired on the job.

—Peter Drucker

Statistics indicate that, as a result of overwork, modern executives are dropping like flies on the nation's golf courses.

—Ira Wallach

EXECUTIVE SUMMARY

leasing your boss is the avenue to promotion. To be successful, scrupulously follow these moves:

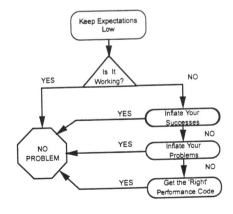

Leader's Guide

A boss who is "with it" performs essential tasks such as coaching (lecturing, nagging, henpecking, harping, browbeating, scolding, and haranguing) and human-resources planning (the dirty work of deciding which human debris will be swept away in the next wave of corporate downsizing). In today's workplace, an employee may wonder about his supervisor, *friend or foe?*

Believe it or not, bosses generally aren't fiends, monsters, or martinets. It's not even mandatory that they be incompetent. They are simply fellow strugglers who may experience the world from a slightly different perspective than you do. For example:

New Boss
If your boss is new to his position, you must have a rear-view mirror . . . and make sure you check it every few hours, perhaps even more often. You see, your new superior will have to establish this dominant verity: he's the boss. He's in charge, so more than likely he will want to start juggling all of the personnel and their positions.

This strategy is based on the need to make the staff squirm and feel ill at ease. It likely indicates a certain percentage of his employees will be canned. But from management's point of view, it seems any new tactic is a sign of progress.

Career Ladder Boss
If your boss has been around longer than most, he is anxious to climb up the corporate ladder (or be put out to pasture with the other old goats).

New bosses like to change things.

For personal vested interests, this type of boss will bust a gut to assemble a loyal team that will support her/his ideas.

Your Personal Goal

Size up this scenario. A big company. A little company. Three executives try to position themselves for the top job. They've spent many years at it, climbing up, around, and over tens, maybe hundreds, of other peers. They got this far. Only one gets it. Usually within a couple of months, the other two are gone. Your goal is to get that promotion. Close counts only in horseshoes and slow dancing. You need to ensure that your boss believes you are a winner.

So How Do You Do It?

Whether your boss is brand-new or has hung around as long as a Galapagos tortoise, he/she will have an immense impact on your career opportunities. Remember: advancement and promotion decisions are made by your boss. (He/she may act as though "the top brass are responsible," but 99 percent of the time your boss is the one.) These scientific decisions are based on subjective evaluation, arbitrary decision, and rolling dice. This is simply the twenty-first century application of the golden rule: "He who has the gold makes the rules."

Your relationship with your boss is a barometer of your potential for success. Brace yourself to shoulder a hefty load of your boss's dirty work. After all, your boss person would rather that you empty the trash and shovel the guano.

A new boss provides you with a superlative

opportunity to conduct an orientation program, as it were, to assist your new leader in becoming acquainted and learning the ropes. Inform your new leader about those devious denizens she/he must watch out for. By doing that you have gotten in like the proverbial Flynn as a valued *insider and confidant.*

Bosses on the move will transfer or axe any deadhead they perceive as a threat. This ensures smooth sailing because no one around will have the moxie to criticize his/her ideas. Ambitious bosses are dead set against leaving any wounded enemies on the field. They avariciously yearn for loyal supporters who promulgate their programs and their virtues. After all, you are an emissary not only for your boss and the company but to the entire corporate world. By going along with his agenda, you position yourself as a colleague and supporter.

There is nothing esoteric about this: You will increase your informal influence if you scrutinize your boss's every word, mannerism, and peccadillo. Remember your boss person is an eagle, so you must watch her/him like a hawk. Learn his likes and dislikes. *Tailor your behavior to* meet your boss's likes. However, be as *different* as is acceptable. You don't want to be labeled a "yes" person or a rubber stamp (even though, for all practical purposes, you may be). If your boss wears only suits, wear suits. But if he seems to like colored shirts, don a bold-colored or striped shirt that demonstrates you are an individual and a dauntless self-starter. Men, wear a bright tie to stand out; women—flashy, unusual jewelry.

Now hear this! Be different only to the degree that is acceptable. For example, use sagacious judgment in choosing your attire for the company picnic. If you work for Warner Brothers, don't wear

Remember, you like what the boss likes.

a Mickey Mouse wristwatch; if you labor for Disney, don't dare wear a Bugs Bunny T-shirt. You want your boss and fellow employees to recognize you as a free thinker who is independent to a point. Yet, you don't want them to shake their heads and mutter, "What an odd duck! What a fruitcake!" You want to identify yourself as a member of the team and in the clubhouse.

Remember: you like what the boss likes. What interests the boss should fascinate the hell out of you. So, if your boss mentions he/she has an aquarium, become an expert on fish.

NOTE. If your boss happens to combine the character traits of Jack the Ripper, Attila the Hun, and Don Rickles—violent rage, aggression, and cynicism—ignore this section and apply for a transfer to another department!

In addition to cultivating your flowering relationship with your boss, merely follow these steps to confirm that your career prospects are suitably enhanced:

First Step: Keep Your Expectations Low

You must always lowball your objectives for the year. After all, it is highly unlikely that your boss will have the foggiest notion whether the six-month project you negotiated can actually come to full bloom in four months. In this manner, when you hand him the completed project in **five** months, he might even grunt, "Snerdly, I thought you were going to finish this in six months. Hmm, you brought this one in early." It's not that difficult to be a hero.

Second Step: Inflate Your Successes

Don't hide your light under a barrel . . . or cover your glow from view. Some people are so modest and self-effacing they are petrified that their fellow staffers will think they're bragging if they chance to highlight the slightest success.

Stare it straight in the face. If you want to achieve, if you want to advance, if you want to leave the timid types in the dust, brag a little. Matter of fact, brag a lot. I remember the immortal admonition of my mom, "Herbie, I've told you a million times not to exaggerate."

So, your status is in whose hands? Yours. If your attitude is positive, you will look like a winner (as though you'd hit 71 HRs, one beyond Mark McGwire's 70). If you think you're a winner, you're a winner.

It's not necessary to announce your accomplishments over the loudspeaker or have them on a marquee outside the main entrance of the building . . . although on occasion you might consider that ilk of showboating.

It is, however, dreadfully important to let your fellow pariahs learn about all you are accomplishing and also scads of fantastic stuff you will accept credit for having done by your own creative, dynamic wits (and half wits). Certainly all for the glory and honor of the company . . . and also to make your superiors shine like Strom Thurmond's hairless pate.

Anyhow, you are sagacious enough to realize that they'll ultimately claim they did it all by themselves, anyhow.

If you accomplish success **outside** of your list of negotiated objectives, aptly remind your boss of your initiative, risk-taking, and mastery of capitalizing on opportunities. By all means, never take responsibility unless it is a **huge success** and always with faked modesty.

Then without fail suggest protracted feedback sessions with your boss when your projects are running *on full*. What an auspicious period merely to confab about how your brilliant concepts are going. Milk it for all it's worth and involve your head honcho in the intricate details of your tactics that forged your successes.

Ah, yes, make sure this impressive news is overly documented with copies for everyone's files. Testimonials from your previously primed sup-porters will more than suffice.

Step Three: Inflate Your Problems

Balance the scales. Even as you exaggerate your stellar accomplishments, you must blow up the first magnitude of the trials and tribulations that, for the sake of the company, you have faithfully and courageously endured.

Festoon your problems as giant and then progressively gargantuan. This will justify the increase in time and resources to give an additional boost to your earth-shattering projects. Underline it three times in red: **no problem is so immense or taxing that it cannot be piled on another fellow struggler.**

Step Four: Arrange for the Right Performance Appraisal Code

With a capital M, you must enter the best possible rating into the computer. Such an extra-ordinary code is assessed by those who are creating and designing the fast-track list, job searches, succession plans, and a glut of variegated career-enhancing opportunities. *The code counts.* May the code be ever before you and with you and around you.

What a pair of twins: the combination of inflating both your problems and successes throughout the year will help ensure that your boss has low performance expectations. Hence, even mediocre, pedestrian performances will appear remarkably good. To clinch your entire scheme with suavity and finesse, withhold the announcement of your gigantic success of the year (preferably the deal your boss' boss yearned for) until shortly before your performance appraisal review with your boss.

During your performance review meeting, naturally your boss will carry you through the predictable ritual of asking you to lay bare your strengths and weaknesses. When going over your strengths, you must trot out testimonials and positive documentation that would make Robert Schuller blush with the knowledge that your positives outweigh all of his!

When queried about weaknesses, meekly admit: "Because I'm a results-oriented team leader, I sometimes push my staff somewhat over deadlines to meet all of our customer commitments. But I'm working on this." Of course, you may always add. "I'm not perfect yet, but I'm always working on that!"

Now that you have the apropos performance code in the computer files, you are in the gateway to the fast track! As your boss commends you for your devotion and dedication to duty, and signs the paperwork for your merit increase, in your mind sing The Eagles' "Life in the Fast Lane."

ACADEMIC SUMMARY

The boss's assessment of the subordinate's performance is based on what the boss believes, makes believe, perceives, construes, misconstrues, and fabricates to constitute an objective evaluation of job performance. The boss cannot elucidate the specificity of the phantasmagorical puzzlements in the upper cavities in his/her cranium since reality cannot be real, so to speak, because the job cannot be defined! A superior perception of what is considered ideal in good practice is subject to distortion by redefining the superior's context of the ideal, as it were.

Get it?

It's important to get the right
Performance Appraisal Code.

2. Working with Turkeys

When his I. Q. reaches 50, he should sell.
—Name Withheld by Request

Here's a good rule of thumb. Too clever is dumb.
—Ogden Nash

He would argue with a signpost.
—R. Dangerfield

EXECUTIVE SUMMARY

Jerks. Dweebs. Dorks. Designations for difficult people existing in the subjunctive mood. One of my favorite appellations is turkey.

Turkeys may be spotted in virtually every office environment, whether you work in the private sector or for a government agency. Turkeys appear in all sizes, shapes, and in at least three sexes. *Their number-one goal in life is to make everybody else's lives miserable—uncomfortable and unpalatable, too.*

Follow this guide for constructive approaches to working under, over, alongside, and hopefully around, these pestiferous birds:

24

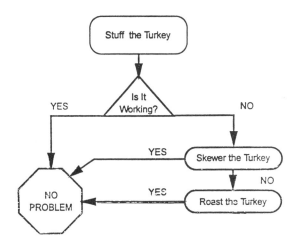

LEADER'S GUIDE

Many different breeds of turkeys roam the workplace. Let me assist you in identifying the garden-variety birds who will gobble, gobble and peck you almost senseless. Perhaps, after this orientation, you can become an accomplished turkey plucker.

The Ego-distended Turkey

This sadistic breed of bird torpedoes your extremely important briefing or presentation the moment you open your mouth. This gobbler pecks before you have had the slightest chance to make your case. Sadly, this jerk can succeed at undermining your argument, causing you to appear ill-prepared and/or incompetent.

Pause to notice how this strain of turkey puffs itself up full of self-importance. This narcissistic bird's antics usually occur in staff meetings, and even occasionally with prime customers or clients. After hijacking your presentation, this self-appointed jackass (or jenny) dearly loves to embarrass you with irrelevant questions and off-topic comments

25

designed to enhance his/her position and make you look bad with a capital B. This cynical contempt for others' ideas is only surpassed by his/her inflated ego. This abrasive personality is perfectly balanced—a chip on each shoulder.

The Gross Ignoramus Turkey

A gross ignoramus is 144 times worse than an ordinary ignoramus. This turkey has two brains: One is lost, and the other is out looking for it. The gates are down and the lights are flashing, but the train isn't coming. This turkey requires 90 minutes to watch *60 Minutes*. This turkey is a prime candidate for natural deselection.

If you give him a penny for his thoughts, he'd owe you change. He sets low personal standards and then consistently fails even to achieve them. He would adore working with you on a project, but he would be out of his depth in a parking-lot puddle. His only redeeming quality, it seems, is he creates superabundant joy when he leaves your office.

The Perky Turkey

You're breaking your neck dashing to an important meeting. Yeah, you're cornered in the hall. You unlucky devil, the perky turkey has caught you. This talkaholic member of the gobbler genus will delay you and any other unsuspecting worker. He or she will ecstatically engage you in useless banter, inane pleasantries, pseudo-business, and a profusion of other light, airy topics to consume your time, impede your efficiency, and make you late. Because of your courtesy, you ordinarily don't tell the perky turkey where to go, although he would

Watch out for the 'Big Mouth' turkey.

roast there.

The Big-mouth Turkey

No matter the subject at hand, this know-it-all bird thinks it has all of the answers. This turkey is stuffed to the giblets with useless advice. This omniscient one is a most annoying bird, to say the least. Every time you and your colleagues open a discussion or address a new problem, this turkey goes gobble, gobble and waddles forth with the *instant answer.* And he'll also go blah, blah, blah until you want to climb the walls.

Not only does this big-mouth prattle non-stop, he will butt in when you want to utter a sound. The standard speech problem of this loudmouth is to say it once, then say it again with different words, and then summarize what he's said. The simplest statement can consume five minutes. No amount of nodding off or futile attempts by others to interrupt can slow down and/or stop this motor-mouth.

The Complainer Turkey

This boring brand of self-absorbed birdbrain can peck at the minutest fault of others. This gobbler will subject you to a distracting sulk-fest about how bad off he/she is. This turkey will squawk, weep, pout, point fingers, make his/her case loudly—and look embarrassingly asinine. This turkey complains to the extent you'd declare it was being sacrificed for a holiday feast. Impossible to ignore, this whimpering bird eventually upsets all those within earshot. Offer this whiner a bit of cheese to complement the whine!

Your Personal Goal

Regardless of the cost, you want to avoid all noxious contact with these demoralizing feathered enemies. You want to disassociate yourself with every genus of turkey. With good fortune, you just might enjoy a little roast turkey.

So How Do You Do It?

Stuff the Turkey

Fight fire with fire. Beat the turkey at his own game. Winning and winning big is what counts. Losing is career-limiting and sure as heck no fun. Here are several strategies for victory in an interchange with one of these birds:

☺ When discussing an issue or a situation that demands resolution—and it doesn't appear to be running in your favor—don't commit to anything. Simply keep on talking. This will create an aura of commitment.

☺ If the turkey still insists on discussing the *real* issue, *elevate the problem to a higher, more abstract plane.* For instance: "The problem is not declining sales. The cogent problem is that the company is not strategically positioned to effectively capture new business opportunities emerging in Eastern Europe." The more you can levitate the discussion to a more ethereal level of abstraction, the better! This ambiguity positions the discussion away from your lousy sales record and forces your bird opponent to defend the lousy Eastern European

29

strategy.

☺ If the turkey is becoming bizarre, spouting outrageous pronouncements and pouring out eccentric ideas, immediately begin to *take notes.* Then feed back the turkey's comments to the turkey himself. So, Ms. or Mr. Turkey will become captive to his own inane assertions. This will stimulate her/his accommodation. The feedback will serve as fast-rising stuffing and will tend to compel the bird's acceptance of your point of view.

☺ If the turkey is pulling a power play by trying to intimidate you, or *snow you—stand up.* Never sit in these circumstances and always have your back to a wall.

If you are losing in the negotiations, it is essential that you buy time. Withdraw from the fray, but only temporarily. Any sort of excuse will suffice. Possibilities include feigning illness, setting your watch alarm to go off as if for an appointment, having a confidant page you or call you on your cellular phone. Throwing up in your lap will work, but it's not recommended if you have a lunch date.

If you are winning in the negotiations, declare victory and deliberately withdraw. Confide in the turkey, asking that bird, "Please, may I count on you to look after my interests?" Chances are the turkey will express eternal gratitude.

Skewer the Turkey

Sooner or later all turkeys skewer them-selves, but you can initiate the process and sauté the bird.

Sure enough the best place for a skewering is a public forum. Here's how you structure a public humiliation that will rid you of the turkey for good:

☺ The first step in preparation for the meeting is to discredit the turkey. Remember that information is power. Seed the grapevine with delicious and mouthwatering rumors. To be fair (and maintain credibility), on occasion even incorporate bits of trivial truth.

☺ Your goal is to *win,* to assure that your point of view, your suggestion, your way gains overwhelming approval in the meeting. To accomplish this you must have allies. So, it is necessary that you laden the meeting with empathetic anti-turkeys, hopefully long before it starts. Never, never, never agree to a meeting until you have a winning alliance in place.

☺ Your winning alliance of supporters will help you spear the turkey and keep it spinning on the rotisserie until all its sides are cooked. *Cut your deals* in advance, enlisting as many allies as possible for your cause. It's better to have the results down pat before you step into the meeting. Let your allies praise you and cheer you on.

Roast the Turkey

If matters are becoming intolerable, and the turkeys are starting to get you down, maybe it is the suitable time to light the fire for a turkey roast.

When drastic action is called for, follow the age-old maxim, "Do unto others before they do it unto you." Now is the propitious time to plot with fellow sufferers to arrange a meeting to discuss these concerns with the boss. Hopefully, other organizational mavens will happily pile on. If your boss remembers the dirty work you've done for him in the past, maybe you can start to say "sayonara" to the turkey.

Of course, it's possible that the turkey is a churlish brute, and your tactics could become slippery. Align yourself with colleagues noted for off-base or abhorrent behavior. Motivate them to lead the revolt. In the event it fails, better their heads than yours!

WARNING: Any misfire of the above tactic could also signal that you may be an emerging turkey!

ACADEMIC SUMMARY

The genus of a workplace pariah defining the character typology we have identified herein as *turkey,* displays a range of counter-productive, self-aggrandizing behavior, including abrasiveness and obstructionism. Here is the suitable coping strategy offering the prospect for the most success in dealing with interpersonally dysfunctional persons: **Shift the paradigm by helping the *bird* to baste** in its own juices!

NOTE: The above theory has been tried only in laboratory conditions. It may not produce similar findings off-campus. Ahem! Gobble! Gobble!

3. Surviving Leadership Training

You can always tell a leader, but you can't tell him much.

—Roger Denton

When the best leader's work is done, the people say, "We did it ourselves."

—Oprah Winfrey

I used to think that anyone doing something "weird" was "weird." I suddenly realized that anyone doing anything "weird" wasn't "weird" at all, and it was the people saying they were "weird" that were "weird."

—Paul McCartney

EXECUTIVE SUMMARY

Companies conduct corporate retreats or leadership conferences in order to create the reassuring impression that the company has sound executive leadership and is on target in developing a talent pool

33

<u>of future leaders.</u> *

Utilize these events to polish your leadership image . . . but keep your eyes wide open. Unless you proceed with the utmost caution, you will become encumbered with utopian visions and useless buzz words. Follow these guides to embellish your extraordinary leadership potential.

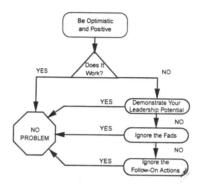

LEADER'S GUIDE

Aha, atop your mail stack, there is a missive addressed to you from your Chief Executive. It becomes necessary for you to plop down somewhere and draw a deep breath. Your company has been downsizing like crazy. With sweaty palms and brow, your paranoid grey matter conjures up visions of insecurity: *Good grief, now*

---

*In the real world, a company retreat can be a very positive experience or a group funk. As a positive, a group leaves with a clear strategic direction and a willingness by team members to support one another to achieve success. Positive retreats are designed to accomplish clear goals and are usually professionally facilitated and well organized—a product of good planning and leadership. The case study in this chapter represents the not-so-successful version of a corporate retreat.

they're gonna make me walk the plank into the sea of professional oblivion!

But, with trembling hands, you open the envelope. Gloryoski, it's not your final notice. No pink slip. It's not even a memo justifying the current "workforce refinement program" (lay-offs). It's an invitation you dare not ignore or refuse: your head honcho summons you to attend a corporate retreat. While you've avoided becoming roadkill on the corporate highway, be wary! A so-called retreat is not necessarily an advance (and in military terms, during a retreat, plenty of once-warm bodies are strewn along the roadway).

These usually annual rituals are conducted far away from the corporate office—in Dry Prong, Louisiana, Tichenor (Ontario, Canada), or Ypsilanti, Michigan (unless your offices are located in one of those sites). And for excellent reason. Executives would be horrified if their minions actually found out what they did or what was being done to them during these costly company camping trips.

Impressive . . . or What?

To the uninitiated, retreats normally resonate their importance—*the competitive-strategy* conference or the *leadership-for-success* seminar—and they are sometimes booked into luxury get-aways such as resorts or expensive conference centers.

Retreats are sometimes not-so-subtle attempts at teaching the corporate mantra to the unindoctrinated. You will spend the next three days of enforced bonding, hearing all about the company's vision, culture, and values.

There once was a time when vision statements weren't necessary <u>because companies were led by visionaries.</u> However, your conference moderator will try and make certain that you memorize this magical statement (the more convoluted the language, the more trouble your company is in).

The company's "core values" are traits the bosses presume you will embrace with every fiber of your being, including integrity, citizenship, honesty, pride in work, desire to learn, and dedication to tasks. Sounds good, doesn't it? Of course, your behavior will be monitored against these noble values.

Now, it's not exactly an initiation into a cult, but it's close enough. It is doubtful whether you be required to take an oath, swearing to spend every waking moment fretting over the company. Anyhow, though, that's the general drift. A chunk of the program will aim for the adjustment of your warped attitude (since you are probably out of sync with the organizational rhythm). Other corporate character-building segments will focus on enhancing your leadership skills to "facilitate the corporate resources re-allocation program" (a fancy-sounding peculiarity for, you guessed it, downsizing).

So, like a good Scout you check into the conference center at Prickly Acres Resort. And you sit obediently at a table behind your name tent. As you size up the participants during the introductions, chills run up and down your spine. Shudder! *These aren't the fast-trackers. Why, these bozos are on the most likely list—the most likely to be canned! So why in hades am I here?* What else can you do but look to your young facilitator named Sherri.

You notice Sherri's pristine good looks and perki-ness. And now, here comes the spiel. At this point you try your hardest not to gag on the rancid breakfast you wolfed down en route. "Our task as leaders is to align our employees' goals with the company vision and to empower them so they can operate to their optimum potential," she intones. You think this sounds like shoveling fog, but you hang tough and request clarification.

"Leadership is a holistic process," she continues, "that is accessed dynamically through all functions of the organization, from the bottom up, to become a management-empowered, team-leadership sharing procedure."

It dawns on you that the split second you <u>process</u> her words, they're gone with the wind, dissipating vapor-like into thin air. If a dense fog enshrouds your frontal lobe immediately thereafter, it will not soon lift. You talk to yourself inwardly, *Hey, maybe this' a propitious time to quit your job and head for a communal farm.* You're not even swayed by the free meals. You probably don't want a hiatus from your significant other. Well, the fact is . . . you'd rather not be here. You must make a conscious decision to serve as an amorphous team player or to get out of Dodge!

Your Personal Goal

Naturally, your overriding goal is to remain on the company leadership high potential list. Believe it or not, you might be able to enjoy the surroundings, tolerate the gibberish, and hasten back to the office ASAP.

So How Do You Do It?

Be Optimistic and Positive

☺ Plaster a broad, toothy grin on your face. A friendly and optimistic demeanor is de rigeur. Avoid looking like a robot from sci-fi. Look the other person in the eye when you speak to her/him and always say her/his name. Play along with warm fuzzies for fellow conferees without cooing and sucking up to the faculty (subtle stroking is permissible, however).

☺ Avoid talking about yourself. Make positive comments about others in the company, even the turkeys. In these booster-ridden forums, pessimism is about as welcome as the annual income-tax form.

37

☺ If the discussion is boring, take notes. Or doodle or do caricatures of the faculty. When you're jotting down points, you don't have to react to the stupid comments of your fellow retreatants.

☺ You may usually expect the company execs to drop in and inquire maternally and/or paternally, "How's it going?" If they ask how the boys and girls are doing at playing in the executive sandbox, simply reply with a straight face: "They are fighting trim, with a song in their hearts and a spirit fit for any fate" (in other words, restructuring).

Demonstrate Your Leadership Potential

Believe me, the protocols for these soirees are taken **very** seriously by the Human Resources staffers who spent months devising them. Each discussion group must appoint a "recorder" and "timekeeper" at the outset. The recorder's first job is to review the Purpose of the session and why all the people present are there ("Jack's from Accounting, and his job is to tell us we can't afford things. Mary has been with the company for twenty-two years, and her role is to tell us how we used to do things around here.") Make sure the recorder understands that your submissive function is to guarantee that any and all workshop recommendations are in alignment with the company's strategic direction. This positions you as a cus-todian, and ardent defender, of the Corporate Vision—a true leader's role.

Enter, ye olde timekeeper. That person gives his/her rules. Those guidelines usually involve allotting a specific number of minutes being assigned to each person who speaks during this discussion session. Let us fondly hope, for your career's sake that you have no last-minute brain-storm when you've exhausted your time.

38

No-Bull Management

Your solid-gold opportunity to showcase your leadership acumen will occur during the teamwork segments of the program. In order to inject a competitive spirit, participants are assigned to teams. They are given names and gain cohesiveness by wearing colorful shirts and hats. Your Gold team will play silly games, hoping to earn sufficient points to beat the Blue and Red teams. During these inane exercises, you will have excellent opportunities to demonstrate your amazing leadership potential. You can lead the cheers vociferously when it's announced that your group has pulled ahead in the standings. "Go Team, Go! Go Gold!"

Then there are those experiential learning gymnastics allegedly designed to enhance leadership and build team *esprit de corps.* These activities, many of which can be out-of-doors, may include the following physical actions: balancing, catching, climbing, crawling, swinging, and walking. For example, a group is blindfolded and asked to hold onto a rope and form a perfect square. Unfortunately, the facilitator has set up a configuration where the group is hopelessly entwined with the rope.

Almost all attendees will do precisely as they're told, no matter how ridiculous the directions they are assigned. (Otherwise, they'd be deemed "uncooperative"). This is where you can tangibly display initiative and risk-taking. Challenge the blindfold rule and implore of the facilitator (friendly and positively, of course), "Please, would you mind explaining how teamwork is learned by wearing these blindfolds?" The facilitator will possibly be stymied . . . and then single you out as a sterling example of one who displays leadership characteristics.

By all means, have your camera (the faster the shutter speed, the better) primed for these adventures. This is mandatory, especially if the event calls for scaling a wall, bungee jumping, or other perilous, near-death experiences. Pictures of these strange ceremonies may serve you handily later.

Experiential learning exercises
are aimed at building team spirit.

Back to the Classroom

Then wend your way back to the classroom, replete with graphs, flip charts, portable chalk board, and a plethora of colored markers. These sessions invariably involve <u>caring</u> and <u>sharing.</u> You separate into buzz groups and return with your team's thoughts on flip charts. What inhibits our organization's effectiveness? Guess what, you can spearhead the discussion to facilitate (another boffo buzz word) the team's figuring this out.

Yes, the correct answer is *improved commun-ications.* Bingo! This answer, of course, applies to any business situation—but, hey, your perceptive leadership capabilities were once again exhibited to show endless potential. And don't forget to highlight the word *communication* on the flip chart with a bright red marker! If your team asks you to synthesize (Wow!) all those unruly sheets of flip-chart paper into a purposeful action plan. No problem! You can distill your plan into one word . . . *communication.*

Ignore the Fads

And on and on and on . . . You will hear a "motivational" peptalk from a spellbinding revivalistic-sounding speaker who will barely remember what company he's "preaching" to.

Next, it's time to hear from the author of the flavor-of-the-month business theory. Attendees will be subjected to the overly simplistic views of an *expert* who will provide sweet, pat answers peddled in orgiastic frenzy on how to motivate and lead employees. These *experts* are usually academics who have never managed a lemonade stand, and whose life experience gyrates around the permissive and easy-going lifestyle of academia.

What are the theories they ballyhoo? We've had

theory X, Y, and Z; top-down and bottom-up management; management grids and management matrix; management by objectives; assertiveness training; sensitivity training; ad infinitum. Some management theorist coins a new buzzword, and in the twinkling of an eye, that word becomes tomorrow's leadership-training agenda.

Do not fall prey to being oversold on non-validated concepts advanced as elixirs—er, snake oil—for instant success. Ignore these gimmicks. Use buzzwords at cocktail parties or in academic journals.

What these famous theorists should be speaking about is: HOW TO EARN $10,000 OR MORE FOR AN APPEARANCE! Now this is an entrepreneurial skill worth learning!

Ignore the Follow-on Actions

Now back to reality. Maybe the giant leap to communal living wouldn't work out anyhow. Besides, your office environment is somewhat better than Alexander Solzhenitsyn's Gulag cell. As John Denver put it, "Gee, it's good to be back home again!" Whew! No more retreats for awhile.

You can hide out briefly and peruse that extensive list of personal development goals and resolutions you *had to* create at the retreat. As you scan your bloated list, you realize it all sounds good—but you have a business to run here. As, one by one, you crumple the pages of your list—and shoot them at your wastebasket-basketball goal—you sigh and wonder how you'll rationalize your numbers shortfall at the next sales conference!

ACADEMIC SUMMARY

"You can transform your leadership style" at the company retreat by "re-engineering yourself, with respect to integration into the holism of the company as an emerging entity. An optimistic outlook and positive commitment to the corporate value structure will demonstrate enhanced leadership skills to implement the corporate vision of integrated power-sharing, percolating up from the bottom."

Doesn't that light your fire?

4. Cultivating Your Image

Absence is usually easier to explain than presence.

—Anonymous

The world is divided into men who accomplish things and those who get all the credit.

—Dave Po Chedley

All human beings have gray little souls, and they all want to rouge them up.

—Maxim Gorky

EXECUTIVE SUMMARY

How many of your corporate associates believe it doesn't make any difference what others think of them? How many of them have received that dreaded notice informing them that they have become "redundant"? Image is oftentimes unfortunately, more important than actual performance. Follow these suggested steps in this image roadmap, and "hip" persons will perceive you as a winner.

44

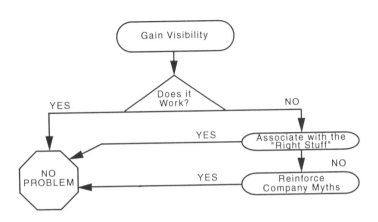

LEADER'S GUIDE

The late Charley Rich sang, "Some gotta win; some gotta lose. Goodtime Charley's got the blues." In business there are two types of players: winners and losers. But in business, unlike pro sports, the hefty bonuses don't always go to the corporate quarterbacks with the highest pass-completion stats or to the hitters with the most RBIs.

Like it or not, merit is often ignored. This is not by choice, however. It's merely that factors such as job objectives, productivity standards, and success criteria frequently aren't gauged because there is difficulty in defining and documenting them. As a result, regardless of the charts—if you are perceived as a winner by the right people—you are a winner. It's that elementary, Dear Watson.

Your Personal Goal

Because the game is downright cryptic, <u>it's how you look, or appear to look, that counts.</u> Your goal, therefore, is for the eyes of the potentates to view you as that *indispensable, special person.*

So How Do You Do It?

☺ *Gain Visibility*

Stare it straight in the face: visibility leads to fortunate breaks and advancement. A low-profile ploy to gain that recognition is to solicit the advice of higher-ups in your organization—even if it's only to authenticate a decision you've already arrived at all by your lonesome. It's ordinarily flattering to the person you've sought out, giving you an entre vous, a subtle platform for self-promotion. Besides, without agreement of your company's moguls your well-laid plans will go *phftt.*

Make yourself well-known to the gatekeepers of valuable information. With changes occurring day by day, rumors flying, and insecurity rife, it is imperative to obtain reliable information. Never underestimate the value of *spies, rumors, and whispers.*

☺ Make Yourself Especially Visible During Holidays

One of the best times to intensify your visibility schemes is during the festive seasons. Select appropriate gifts with care. The basic principle for giving a *little something* during the holidays is: give to those who can help you look good. They will appreciate your thoughtfulness and, of course, remember it.

☺ Here's a Suggested List:

✓ **the editor of the company newsletter;**

46

✓the staff of the Human Resources
   Department who oversee severance
   payments and succession planning;
✓the travel agent;
✓the conference coordinator;
✓*anybody* who generates numbers
✓anybody who receives numbers.

Special Note. Be absolutely certain your secretary and your boss' secretary are on the list. Secretaries are the custodians of the office grapevine. After all, they aren't called SECRETaries for nothing!

☺ Deck *Your* Halls

The merry Christmas season drops an unparalleled opportunity right into your lap. The company Christmas party allows you to shine with the brass around the buffet table and the punch-bowl. As you smile and schmooze, rivet these *rules of misconduct* in mind to ensure that you don't palaver all the way from the middle to the bottom—then to the gutter, and finally down the drain.

☺ Always wear a gaudy Santa Claus tie with flashing lights (if a man) or a huge headband that props up ersatz mistletoe over your head (if a woman). Remember, statistics show that 40 percent of your party-goers are at least partially color blind . . . and you must be noticed at all cost and against all odds.

☺ Always have jokes and hilarious stories on tap, just in case there's a lull in the conversation. Jokes about blondes, interns, and politicians are exceptional crowd pleasers!

Not a good idea.

☺ Always become inebriated so you can call your boss aside and candidly tell him/her what's really been on your mind all along. Do this while smoking a cigar. This is especially effective if you are a woman dressed in a classic suit like Ingrid Bergman in *Casablanca.* And, oh, remember to regurgitate later.

☺ Always sing and dance. The louder you sing, the more impressed people will be. Always do the latest dance craze and organize a revival of the Macarena and the Bunny Hop. You will also merit extra brownie points for being the first person to wear a lampshade on your noggin while you dance the Hokey-Pokey and make a pass at your boss's wife/husband.

Associate with the "Right Stuff"

You absolutely must hob nob with the right persons in the right locations. You can pile up points by keeping your boss posted about how you've exploited (That's the verb!) these occasions to support his/her ideas. (Promotions are granted to team players who can sell their boss' remarkable ideas without shaking all other players off their rungs on the ladder.) These are the "in" people you should butter up:

☺ Spend time with those who can influence your performance appraisal. Ordinarily, these individuals are usually members of your boss' peer group. Cultivate their willingness to provide testimonials.

☺ Appear regularly in the company of

highflyers and *rising stars.* Observers will invariably recognize you as *one of them.*

☺ Always attend a few meetings with *big names* from other companies, significant associations, or government agencies. Then drop their names in conversation referring to each *big name* as "my colleague." Also, it is very impressive to be called out of a meeting or paged in a public forum by a senior company executive or other *big name.* A trusted confidant on your Christmas gift list could probably make the arrangement.

REINFORCE COMPANY MYTHS

You are known by the company you keep and the stories you tell. Your reputation as a team player will not be heightened if you keep pointing out those inconsistencies in the corporate mission statement about how we are a *people-oriented* company.

Now, you are already aware of this, but bosses have an amazing penchant for rewriting history. So stay awake when your boss tells her/his favorite story about how she/he salvaged and rejuvenated the moribund operation inherited from that brain-dead predecessor who had done nothing! Nada! Zilch! Zero! Yawn! You've heard all this before . . . and before that . . . However, supporting this mythology will earn you a passel of brownie points and make you look . . . fantastic.

ACADEMIC SUMMARY

Our theory is that significant interfaces will amplify your image.

Note on Research Model: In capsule form, we assembled data from the reactions of a pertinent, representative sample of business practitioners, of course following the establishment of steering committees to ascertain specifically what it was we were engaged in uncovering. Having accomplished the task of combining several varietal ideas through committee structure, we were in a significantly more empowered position to facilitate a research model we deemed compatible both with those we wished to use as an information resource and certainly in a format that would ease the compilation of data. The results have been a propitious coincidence in that they reflect in gigantic proportions the initial concept of the solution. In effect, our study irrefutably proved our theory!

5. Guarding Against Re-engineering
(and other forms of Corporate Capital Punishment)

Whenever embarking upon "change," remember . . . Never try to teach a pig to sing . . . it wastes your time and annoys the pig.

—*Harold McAlindon*

If you can't change the people, you change the people."

—*Wes Terryberry*

Re-engineering" is especially adaptable to higher levels of management where possible undesirable side effects such as lowered productivity are of little consequence.

—*Doug Roth*

EXECUTIVE SUMMARY

The marketplace is always experiencing rapid and significant changes. Without fail, senior management will exhort you to *get involved* in the process of inaugurating changes, supposedly to ensure that your operation acclimates to new conditions and that it remains viable.

You guessed it already. Your bosses will usher in a new *Program* to assure that you will *re-engineer your department.* Be not dismayed, for you will be able to detain this initiative by following these easy, but also circuitous, guidelines:

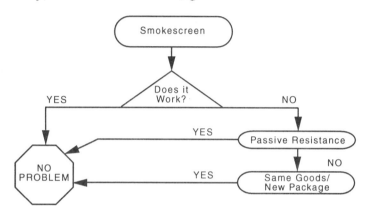

LEADER'S GUIDE

Your Head Honcho will call together the rank and file, including middle and lower management (if any of them remain), for the annual state-of-the-company message. That honcho will ladle out heaping portions of pompous folderol about how "today's tempestuous business climate will mandate the facing and implementation of innovative *changes* and *challenges.*"

And you lucky peons will hear a litany of dishwatery clichés about . . . globalization . . . free trade . . . changing customer needs . . . government cutbacks . . . increased competition . . . emerging technologies—and about how sluggish and bureaucratic departments will not be "Stayin' Alive," as the BeeGees might have chirped it.

On the heels of that pessimistic presentation,

your Chief Bean-counter will sally forth and wail that "the competition is eating our lunch." Gad, no wonder you're hungry. Then to make sure that the gloom is pervasive, Bean-counter will emphatically assert: "We expect you to promulgate ways and means of having fewer lower-level bosses with less avenues of *delaying* and *diluting decisions*—and less *fuzziness* and *fat*.

As a migraine meanders across your mind you are told the "good news." Management has contracted a consulting firm to install *"Process Re-engineering.* "This will enable you to accomplish your task." And it is even better than *Total Quality Management!* And much better than "Quality Circles." The migraine has now become massive.

So, you log your time in a two-day seminar on the why and how of re-engineering. This management dogma embraces the idea that corporate hierarchies should be obliterated and replaced with streamlined "process teams" com-posed of marketing, manufacturing, and sales and service people who employ computers to combine tasks that work without many supervisors.

But what your management guru deliberately did not reveal is that these programs oftentimes create a most nasty scenario. As these changes—sometimes merely for the sake of change—are put into effect, employee anxiety induces chaos and panic. As a result productivity plunges **d**

                              o

                                  w

                                  n

                                    w

                                      a

                                        r

                                        d

Be protective of your resources.

As management responds with a corresponding panic, and frantically insists on eliminating certain positions, **this could include yours!** The impending danger is that *you* could be sideswiped in *collateral* damage . . . and it's impossible to unscramble an egg.

Your Personal Goal

Manifestly, your goal is to keep your turf intact.

So How Do You Do It?

Stockpile Resources
Always anticipate management's next big thing, because it can cause you considerable heartburn.

Make imperative precautionary moves before programs like re-engineering are off and running. Constantly develop creative projects and build up staff to superintend them. Underline this in your private planner: **My real success will be directly related to how large and extensive an empire I can build.**

What's the immediate benefit? An increase in your pay grade because of the larger staff you will supervise and, in the long term, you have acquired insurance against any future hacking and re-rearranging.

Engage in Benign Neglect
As directions to implement this latest organization change effort begin filtering down the company pipeline, you can help institutional second-

guessing to set in. As Niccolo Machiavelli, the hard-nosed author of *The Prince*, contended, the odds are in your favor.

> There is nothing more difficult to carry out, nor more doubtful of success, nor more dangerous to manage, than to initiate a new order of things.
>
> For the initiator has the enmity of all who would profit by the preservation of the old system and merely lukewarm defenders in those who would gain by the new one.

If you are pressured to become actively involved, seek further clarification. Suggest a meeting to study the issues in more detail. Also encourage your colleagues to ask all sorts of questions. As meetings, study groups, task forces and reports multiply, the top brass will view you as contributing to teamwork, consensus seeking, and change making.

So, what'll happen? Eventually, managers at every level will *delay* and *dilute* until the original purpose is so nebulous, not a soul is sure exactly what senior management wanted. Here are further ploys that will provide cover for your haunches:

☺ If asked for proof of results, seriously report that there is no considerable progress as yet, but the various planning meetings are well attended.

If pushed by the higher ups, assure senior management that your employees are dedicated and devoted (to constructing their own coffins!). "They're really into it!"

☺ And as you make your report, it is imperative for your seniors to notice that you look like the *ideal* **agent of change.** (Be sure to *change* your hairstyle, wardrobe, significant other, whatever). You do not want to be perceived as someone who resists change (That is definitely career limiting.)

☺ To assure that the re-engineering will die a natural death, recognize from the word go the typical pattern for the introduction of these "re-whatever" programs. After the release of each new faddish, best-selling book, management types will go ga ga. *In Search of Excellence, Organization Renewal, Quality Circles, Total Quality Management, Process Re-engineering,* ad infinitum. Every seemingly new concept will assure you gargantuan cost savings and "quantum leaps" in efficiency and performance. La de da.

If you tried on each and every new layer of the new management "apparel," you would begin to resemble an urchin, aimlessly plodding the streets, hopelessly overdressed for the season—not unlike Cyndi Lauper—and also crying out for a delousing and head-to-toe cleansing! Ah, but you can become clean. These quick-fix programs are only an interim transformation en route to Standard and Poors.

But, maybe not all of this posturing is negative. Perhaps part of it is even refreshing. However, if management truly wants to save the company, calling in the new "in" author with the "coolest" (or hottest, however you describe it) management fad is akin to summoning a pyro-maniac to extinguish a fire!

☺ Remember that "this, too, shall pass." Many of the concepts are incomplete ideas. Most employees already have grasped the answer to, "What's in it for me?" The reward systems to support these cure-alls are seldom put in place. While employees seem to enjoy serving time on high-performance teams, they notice that these miniature think tanks gradually shrink. Unfortunate-ly, the customers become insignificant in each hectic exercise. And managers forget that changing the mechanics of how people work calls for far more than re-engineering.

As this novel management panacea runs its natural course, you can make several strategic actions to speed up the death throes. You can facilely discredit the program by purchasing a copy of an even more recent book. Then you can distribute summaries to your management team. Attach this note: *This is the cutting edge and makes the current program passé.*

Make a Sacrifice

☺ If you are actually held accountable to demonstrate concrete results—no problem! Here is where you pull out your *wild card.* Make your contribution . . . by sacrificing a part of the superfluous staff you built up. In addition, you will also fortify the fact that you are a team player by relinquishing the budgets tied to the useless projects.

ACADEMIC SUMMARY

The new transformation paradigm insists that the organization re-invent itself by throwing from the train the baggage that inhibits achievement of integrated organizational agility and streamlined administrative processes.

NOTE: This stratagem is at this moment being field tested in three business schools in a double-blind crossover study. Early findings reveal the following trends:

☺ The decimation of the drones returned elephantine profits, allowing the companies to spruce themselves up for a quick sell-off.

☺ That resulted in top management and the author of the re-engineering fad book becoming exorbitantly rich.

We warn that the long-term trends are not yet in . . . **because these companies appear to have gone bankrupt!!!**

6. Coping with Political Correctness

When they say, "Results are being quantified," what it means is, "We're massaging the numbers so they will agree with our conclusions."

—Lorne Plunkett

Don't send a boy to do a man's job these days; send a woman.

—B. Walters

When they say, "We will set up a task force to review . . ." what it means is that seven people who are incompetent at their regular jobs have been loaned to the project.

—Watergate Plumbers

GP (General Practitioner) has now evolved into PC for Primary Care physician. Years ago the PC was simply referred to as a family doctor. What else does PC imply? During World War II, it meant "Privileged Character," a military and/or political person the average grunt was supposed to fawn over with obeisance. Since about 1974 it has often stood for "Personal Computer."

But the PC my feverish brain zeroes in on is the panacea to end all panaceas . . . that coverall device called POLITICAL CORRECTNESS! The No Bull Manager must tread softly, or he will step smack-dab into the middle of a quagmire. Put on your hip-boot waders, friends.

EXECUTIVE SUMMARY

The No-Bull Manager does not strive to be politically correct. Otherwise, he would be the Full-of-Bull Manager. The Manager who yearns for unsoiled feet recognizes that he must navigate the shark-infested waters of the "politically correct" organization. Simply follow these politician-tested guidelines:

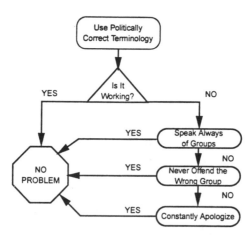

THE LEADER'S GUIDE

It's coming at you thick and fast—multi-culturalism, diversity, employment equity, women's issues, sexual identity flaps, harassment, ad naus-eam. Unless you trip the "light fantastic toe" (John Milton), you run the risk of being labeled a racist, sexist, homophobic, Texas-Chain-Saw-Massacre madman (er, madperson, excuse me)—or even worse!!! If you dare demonstrate naïvete in these areas, you will become a sitting (and lame) duck in most of the viciously competitive organizations. And you might be routed, toasted, whipped, and marked for the zilch file. There is the distinct possibility that certain "in" persons may perceive you as an unsavory remnant of an earlier age: BPC—Before Politically Correct.

Frankly, whoever started hatching up all of this PC stuff should be publicly pilloried and perhaps tarred and feathered . . . but that assuredly wouldn't be at all politically correct, unless it were being meted out on those who are politically incorrect ala Salem, Massachusetts, ca. 1692.

Your Personal Goal

Uh huh, your goal, is not only to survive in today's politically correct organization, but also to thrive. A measure of your success will lie in your astuteness at surfing through the English language (or even Spanish, French, Japanese, Chinese [all dialects],Yoruba, Swahili, or Arabic), employing verbiage that inflates and bolsters all those you encounter, or may encounter, in the modern organization, whether minnow, whale, or blowfish.

SO HOW DO YOU DO IT???

Merely listen to the "doublespeak" of the average politician. Hey, the mastery of political

No-Bull Management

correctness is a virtual snap. Learn a few key terms like *diversity* and *glass ceiling*. Then you'll become a consummate spin doctor in your own right. And you'll probably manage to keep your footsies clean!

Always Use Politically Correct Lingo

In the course of human events, and even in normal (what's normal anymore?) conversation, you may inadvertently offend an overseas rep to Lower Slobbovia who may lodge a complaint against you with the corporate human rights commissioners, harassment officers, employment equity police, and others operating in the service of grievance bearers with ever-expanding lists of claims on beaucoup of others.

It is absolutely vital for you to articulate your feelings when communicating with your colleagues. But you positively must understand and employ the correct codes. Thus, proper exchange of ideas and information can continue without complaint, which is nigh onto impossible, but anyhow . . . Speak carefully, daintily, mincingly, and <u>correctly</u>, of course. Practice these in front of a mirror while emoting a pained expression—similar to that elicited by hemorrhoids—that virtually screams, "I feel your pain!"

Old PI Phrase
☺1. Do it and do it now.
☺2. Do it right, or you're fired.
☺3. Your plan sucks.

☺4. He's a jerk-dweeb-dork-South end of a jackass

New PC Phrase
☺1. Can you sign up for this program?
☺2. I'm confident you'll get it done.
☺3. Let me share my feelings on this.
☺4. He's simply not committed to what we're trying to

heading North.
☺5.Stick it where the sun don't shine.
☺6.His head is up his rear.
☺7.This job is like a term in a Nazi concentration camp.
☺8.He's unemployed.

accomplish.
☺5.Thank you for your needed input.
☺6.He suffers from retro-cranial trouble.
☺7.I exult in a challenge.

☺.8.He's a consultant.

It's Always GROUP Therapy . . . Whatever

Have you heard the nostalgic song about "Just Mollie and me, and baby makes three. We're happy in my Blue Heaven"? How politically incorrect! You know that "It Takes a Village" to rear a child or do most anything. That's why there are so many politically correct experts with their pristine little hands in nearly everything we do.

Always refer to groups and not individuals. Categorize, box, and label every Tom, Dick, and Harriet. Don't even think about individuality. I mean, we are all part and parcel of this amorphous mass of PCness. That's why the individual is anathema to the currently correct slant on history, society, organization studies, and the general nature of the late Carl Sagan's universe. We must interpret everything in terms of groups, especially groups defined by race, gender, class, sexual orientation, management, and unions.

Be careful not to use terminology that a group could find offensive. Never call a "sanitary engineer" a garbage collector! The following PC phrases illustrate the correct terms we must employ (see page 67):

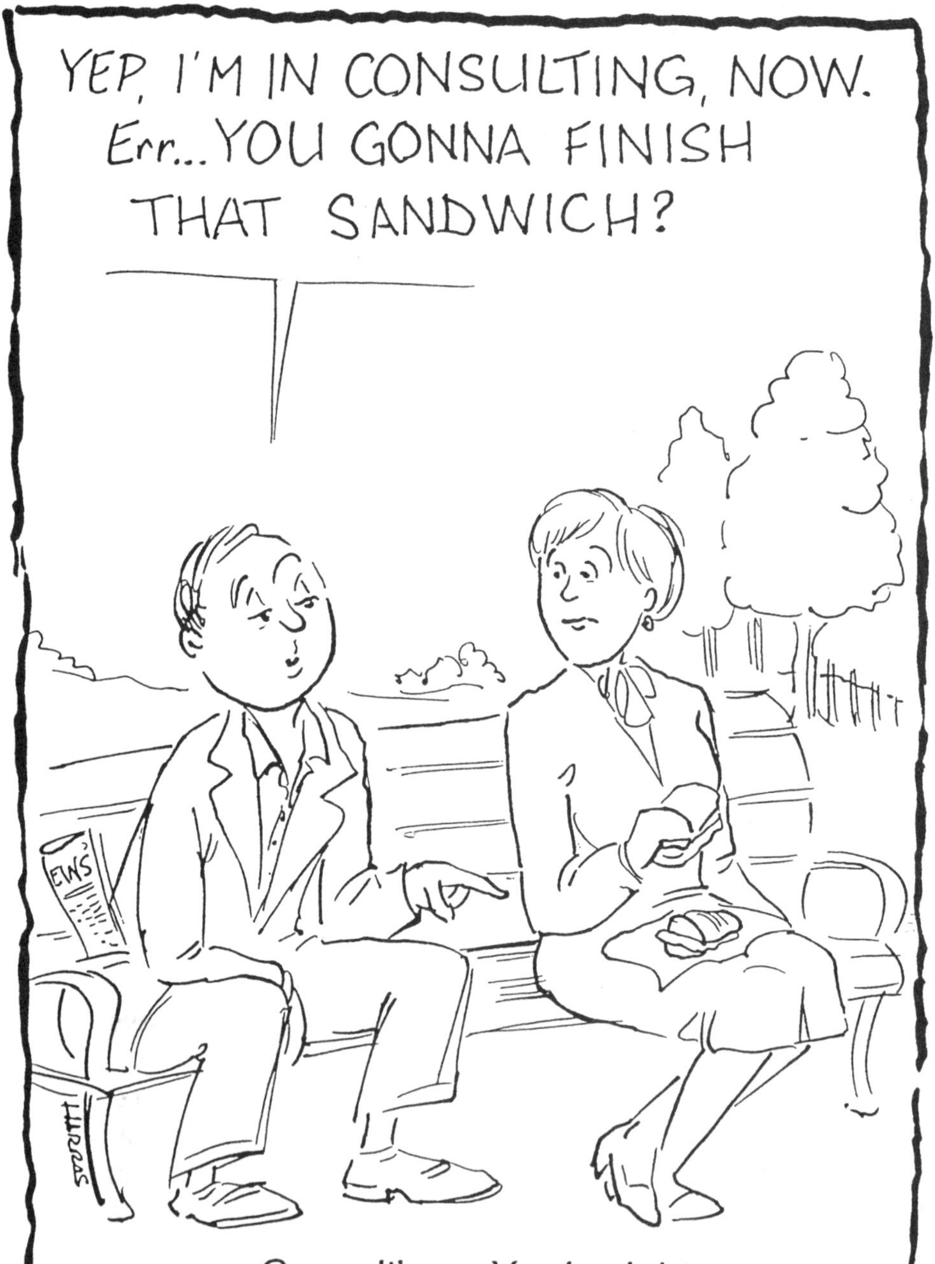

Consulting. Yeah, right.

No-Bull Management

Old PI Terms	New PC Terms
☺Deaf	☺Aurally challenged
☺Old	☺Chronologically challenged
☺Tall or short	☺Vertically inconvenienced
☺Fat	☺Horizontally inconvenienced
☺White	☺Melanin deficient
☺Addicts	☺Chemically inconvenienced
☺Losers	☺Individuals with temporarily unmet objectives
☺Dead	☺Terminally inconvenienced
☺Psychotics	☺Socially misaligned
☺Healthy	☺Temporarily non-disabled
☺Stupid	☺Intellectually challenged
☺Ugly	☺Appearance impaired
☺Bald	☺Follically challenged

Special Cautions

Remember that bruised persons are always innocent victims of oppressive groups, i.e., parents, corporations, teachers, unions, sexists, managers, governments, and churches. It is perfectly accept-able and reasonable that these poor victims should make proverbial mountains out of molehills, turning annoyances into full-scale assaults. Bear in mind that any unintended "insult" is fair game for a lawsuit, a placard parade, a grievance, or a gender

Never offend the wrong group.

equity malfeasance.

The PC approach is to avoid altogether the slightest mention of the individual, particularly the far-fetched notions of individual rights and individual responsibilities. Chronic victims ought (How impertinent to suggest that anyone *ought* do anything!) to learn the lyrics of "Don't Blame Me" and "Put the Blame on Mame, Boys," 'cause they neither take the blame nor the responsibility. "The devil made me do it," Geraldine (a.k.a. the late Flip Wilson) used to alibi, but "she" cooperated with ole Jack Flash.

For example, if George scores poorly in your performance appraisal program, the organization, the union, the supervision, and the system are deliberately failing George. The possibility that the blame for performance lies with the employee is patently inadmissible. Why, that would put the blame on the poor, distraught victim!!!

NOTE: If you are the supervisor, George probably has a good point.

Let's rewrite "Everybody Loves Somebody Sometime" and rename it "Everybody Is a Victim Sometime" (in fact, all the time). Those who think they have been unduly victimized by fate as too poor, fat, thin, tall, short, incompetent, whatever, have a right to demand redress.

Isn't it marvelous to be "trendy"? Eat at trendy cafes? Wear trendy threads? Be totally chic and "in" and all of that rot? But watch for these trends. These "professional victims" will exercise their "rights."

One of them appeared before a judge. The black-robed authority figure inquired, "What rights do you have in mind?" The victim replied, "I don't know, but I demand 'em right here and now!" And they'll exercise them *right in your office—in a group*. They'll demand pity, recompense, compensation, and an apology. In their avidity to further their case, they'll develop an intransigence, presenting threats, demands, ultimatums, deadlines, blackmail, boy-cotts, confrontations, and pour it on. Have a nice day!

Protect your derriere. How? Repeat to yourself at least once an hour: "Group culture is everything. Group culture is everything . . ." Write it on a 3 x 5 card and paste it in a prominent place. Individuals are molded by group culture and are victims of group societal oppression. If matters do not work out copacetically, the fault is not yours. It's everyone else's fault. We're victims! Therefore, we must wear the badge of victimdom . . . and do it with mock humility, backed up by a lawyer.

Never Offend the Wrong Group

Never, ever, criticize any group that is not a part of the oppressor class. You are always on safe ground if you lowrate PI (politically incorrect) groups.

Like most general principles, this rule cannot flawlessly cover all complex situations in sensitive matters such as gender, race, sexual affinity, or ecology. So, you are asked for your opinion on pay equity. You must tiptoe fastidiously. Remaining silent is a good bet, but you want your minions to perceive you as a leader. So, what do you do? Remember that the politically correct brigade will label any argument against their prevailing code as shockingly unthinkable. And no doubt you will be accused of being sexist, racist, ignorant, and offensive. No deviation from the perceived authentic PC Gospel will be tolerated.

No-Bull Management

The Human Resources Task Force, headed by your boss, waits patiently for your reply. Naturally, you believe in equal pay for equal work and that women should be paid the same as men. But this is not the question. The issue is: Should entirely different occupational groups be paid the same? Is a secretary of "equal value" to a truck driver? A clerk to a janitor? Is the heavy lifting of a stevedore as demanding as the continuing-education requirement for a nurse?

You surely are aware that no ordinary mortal should endeavor to answer such questions, but you don't want to be branded as a nitwit by those of any importance.

You are confronted with a dilemma. If your response is not the one you necessarily believe in your heart—but is simply inoffensive and placates the people around you—then it's all a load of bull excrement. Or you can be politically correct and follow the basic rule of deflecting the issue negatively against an oppressor group. You could discuss the historic oppression of the dominating white male heterosexual "ruling class." Or you could denounce that parade of characters, politicians, dupes, and con artists at the Corporate Office that produced this unintelligible, disorganized, socio-legal-techno-pseudo-science.

If you are in a particularly unfamiliar and confusing situation, you can always remain silent and smile (or look stern, depending on the circumstances), but make sure to have a few snappy generalities ready to parry any suspicions. Safe and effective are any positive statements involving the words *diversity, multicultural, ethnicity, disadvantaged groups, knowledgeable, inclusive, and marginalized.*

CONSTANTLY APOLOGIZE!

Being politically correct means always having to say you're sorry. Oh, apologies to Erich Segal, the author of *Love Story*. If your gene pool is made up from an oppressor category, constantly apologize for what your group has done to others. Always castigate yourself for your own disabilities (any position of authority in any organization, male, heterosexual, and in certain cases, able-bodied or intelligent). This display of guilt and humility is extremely valuable if you want to survive. Flaggelate yourself without fail . . . and do it constantly.

This rule is absolutely inviolate in any company meeting. If the topic should digress to topics such as the philosophy of fast-tracking targeted groups via special career assignments, this is an apropos time to make that important phone call. If every eye is turned upon you and anxiously anticipating your comments, mumble shibboleths about past injustices and immediately head to the washroom. You won't miss anything because the conclusion will be about as surprising as the recipe for boiled eggs.

ACADEMIC SUMMARY

Any deviation from orthodox politically correct dogma is anathema to the unforgiving, thought-control constabulary. Revisionist views will be silenced unless you engage in proper thinking and exchange ideas and information in appropriate PC language.

Wow! Now you're occupationally challenged!

7. Surviving Downsizing
(and Your Next Reorganization)

The success of our downsizing program can be attributed to our leaders' latent masochistic tendencies.
—Name withheld upon request

If your job is secure, it's because no one else wants it.
—John Seufert

The view changes only for the lead dog.
—Sergeant Preston of the Yukon

EXECUTIVE SUMMARY

Objective decision-making about who goes and who stays during downsizing is more the exception than the rule. The following hints for survival—patently **your survival**—will assist you in appearing to fit in with the corporate culture, whether or not you indeed do. They will help you avoid the *Managerial Chainsaw Massacre.*

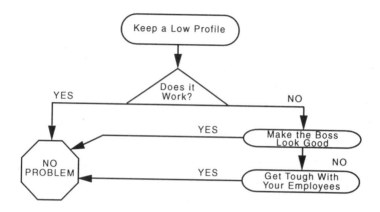

LEADER'S GUIDE

You cannot escape it. Business is lousy, so management must make more profit. This is nothing new. When there's a general downturn in inflow, over against an upturn in outflow, you may as well anticipate a furious rash of job-cutting reorganizations. Executives who are driven by quarterly results become teed off by decreased cash flow, institutionalized second-guessing, organizational sluggishness and lack of bonuses (primarily the scarcity of bonuses). So, the company's generals insist on *surgical sieges.* That means brandishing the executive machetes to hack through the underbrush in pursuit of profit maximization.

In order to understand the terminology you will hear bandied about, here are the correct translations:

"Outsourcing" .... **Downsizing**
"Consulting Help .... **Downsizing**
"Re-engineering .... **Downsizing**
"Total Quality Organization"...... **Downsizing**
"Empowerment" .... **Downsizing**

"Organizational Renewal".......... **Downsizing**

Your Personal Goal

If conditions are tough (and they are at least half of the time), companies will downsize and use draconian tactics. IBM, "Big Blue," coined the clever doublespeak term, *Management Initiated Attrition.* namely, "You bosses fire 'em." Hear ye, hear ye! Your goal is to survive. You don't want to be lumped under the designation of MIA. Until an unparalleled opportunity presents itself, you want to hang onto your position in rough, tough times and elude your being platooned in the unceremonious parade of the unemployed.

So How Do You Do It?

Downsizing affords an all-too-tempting opportunity for managers to dispose of those they dislike or consider a threat. Because of the large number of people involved and the necessary rush, rush, rush, there is virtually no control over the criteria for dismissal. By old-fashioned standards, it's usually impersonal, unfeeling, and downright cruel. It can be as perfunctory as: "Clean out your desk by this afternoon."

You might as well expect downsizing to bring out the worst behavior in the decision-makers.

Here is your game plan. Immediately slide into this survival mode at the first hint of consultants meeting with your chief executives in the *war room.* The following tried and true, real-world tactics may help you be seen by the powers that be as a team player who is worth keeping on the team.

☺ *Keep a Low Profile*

During this gut-wrenching period, you must

75

Make sure your boss knows
how hard you work.

keep a profile as low as a snake's belly and stay out of trouble. It is not the time to stir up a brouhaha or take a stand on anything. Bypass projects or activities that involve controversy, contention, or real or perceived progress. Regardless of a project's potential—and the possible gold at the end of the rainbow—you cannot afford to alienate anyone. Allow others to stick their necks out and become swept away in conflict.

If conflict does rear its hideous head (or if you sense that it is coming), set up a high-level confab out of town, if at all possible. After all, it's more difficult to hit a moving target. Why, that's not running away! Oh, maybe it is, but it's still a ---- sight better than being in the line of fire!

Before you depart for your strategic out-of-town conference, advise those involved in controversy: "Look, I'm not pleased with the situation. When I return, I'll want a full report to make sure that you have resolved this unpleasant development. I'll bank on it!"

You can have your aide or assistant deal with the others to arrange a propitious meeting time when you come back. In that manner, if the situation worsens, you were not involved. You were out tending to the business priorities of the company. If all goes well, obviously your mandate to resolve the problem galvanized the others to swift action. Ah, yes, your leadership acumen comes to the fore again.

If it's necessary for you to stay at the office, report to your associates that you're slaving away 75 hours a week. It is appropriate to look worn out from always hastening to this or that appointment or meeting in a feverish frenzy. Invariably carry an important document and have sweaty armpits. Drop phrases such as "I called the client at 9 last night

. . ." or "When I came in at 5:30 this morning. . . ." And make sure your boss is mindful that you are strapped to cell phones and beepers. When you do leave for home, tote a briefcase the size of a garment bag. Endeavor not to become frustrated because you could probably accomplish your job in a 9-to-5 day.

This is not the time to challenge any facet of company policy. Since you are a self-starting go getter, this will summon the utmost self-discipline from you. Leaders of big companies are normally far removed from the rank and file. They can make an abundance of dumb decisions—and they can formulate some weird policies.

BUT, REMEMBER, YOU ARE A TEAM PLAYER. POLICY IS POLICY. THAT'S YOUR LINE, AND YOU'RE STAYING WITH IT. DON'T LET CONCRETE, TANGIBLE FACTS IMPEDE THE REALITY OF A DUMB POLICY.

☺ *Always Make the Boss Look Good*

It's hell to work for a nervous boss, especially if you're the culprit who's making him nervous. In these days of slash and burn, what your boss cannot tolerate is a threat. Remember, *Your boss is always right.*

Never dispute the boss' decisions, recommendations, or behavior, even if they are downright destructive for the company. This is eminently true in meetings. Bottom-up suggestions proposed in a public forum are quite often seen by bosses as no-confidence votes. You'd better ask the boss a "slow-pitch" question that will make her/him look sharp and highly intelligent.

Never outshine your boss. If you're Tiger Woods, Jack Nicklaus, and Arnold Palmer all rolled into one, let the boss have all the "gimmes" she desires. Be careful not to perform too well in areas of expertise held in common with your boss. Upstaging on that joint presentation with your boss before the executive committee will do nothing to ingratiate your boss to you. Your outstanding effort of doing nothing (or very little) in this situation will be remembered.

Tiger-Jack-Arnold, your valiant efforts will be appreciated.

NOTE: If your boss is in trouble, ignore this section and distance yourself.

If you have even one grand idea, let the boss steal it and take full credit for it. Bosses exist largely to steal their subordinates' best ideas. That's one prime reason bosses become bosses. For example, if you shovel your boss tremendous ideas on how to improve profitability during these trying times, you're fueling your boss' success and . . . prolonging your career. And don't fret and mope if your boss claims your choicest idea as her/his own. A type of revisionist reasoning tends to occur as *your idea* becomes our idea and goes full tilt to become the boss' brainstorm.

☺ *Get Tough with Your Employees*

If you have people working under your supervision, turn all of the aggression and scrutiny on them that is humanly possible. In your boss' jaded eyes, this will make you seem *tough* and *demanding.* You're a snarling, vicious pit bull and "meaner than a junkyard dog," to quote the late Jim Croce. Exactly the kind of executive animal called on to make difficult decisions.

Actually, there is no necessity for your experiencing the "joys of downsizing." Egalitarian-ism is marvelous in theory until it's your livelihood, and head, on the chopping block. In the Wild West they used to comment, "There ain't nothin' like a hangin' to focus the mind."

ACADEMIC SURVEY

To avoid being listed as Management-Initiated Attrition, anticipate involuntary people-reduction through downsizing, rightsizing, upside downsizing, or rightside upsizing. Adopt blatant ambiguous stratagems to reinvent yourself and thus be able to escape the entire enterprise as its falls in around your ears.

8. Selling Your Ideas

Half of the money I spend advertising is wasted; the trouble is I don't know which half.

—John Wannamaker

Don't sell the steak. Sell the sizzle.

—Leota Embleton

Do not open mouth until brain is in gear.

—Anonymous

EXECUTIVE SUMMARY

Leaders who can effectively sell innovative (and, of course, profitable) ideas—no matter how far-out and impractical—are noticed by their peers and superiors. Any Bob and Carol and Ted and Alice can point you toward a new vista . . . but only a minute percentage can steer you there. The following step-by-step primer will aid you in selling your proposals and in winning.

81

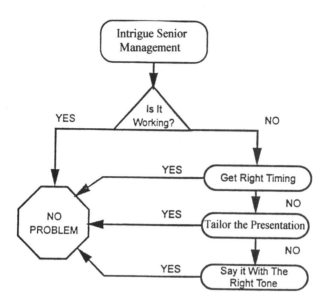

LEADER'S GUIDE

Eureka, you have an earth-shattering idea. But your firm, like most monolithic outfits, is idea-resistant. Right off the bat, all up and down the line, common impedimenta will stymie, stifle, and strangle you. You'll hear, "Well, we've never done it that way before!" or, "That dog won't hunt!" or, "If it ain't broke, why fix it?" or, "It wasn't invented here."

Or, you will be frustrated by the "let's-postpone-and-study-some-more" syndrome. That fear-of-change fixation has aborted innumerable incredible ideas. If you cannot break through those dumb barriers, it's likely you can't make much of a contribution to the team. Sometimes inability to sell your ideas to the key shakers and movers testifies more about your resourcefulness than about the idea itself.

NOTE: If this rings true, reread the chapter on Turkeys.

Pull out all the stops when you're working on a presentation to the management team.

YOUR PERSONAL GOAL

Your personal goal in "mission possible" is to capitalize on this direct correlation between triumphantly selling your ideas (even if with smoke and mirrors) and career elevation.

So How Do You Do It?

Somehow you knew I was going to ask that, didn't you? Your hearers should not have to suffer with toxic nausea after being exposed to one of your petrifying presentations. Do you remember the E. F. Hutton TV commercials that ended with "When E. F. Hutton speaks, everyone listens"? When you speak, you want everyone to listen. Successful selling calls for your personal best, not unprepared, disjointed rambling punctuated with "and ers" and "ahems" and "uhs."

Intrigue Senior Management

You have to locate and press precisely the right buttons to market your one-in-a-million proposal—and you don't even have to directly use the words *bonus, perks,* and *promotion.*

1. Your hook lies in implying, as Dupont Chemical does, "Good things through . . . " You won't speak these exact words, but anybody but a cretin will readily recognize that you're subliminally saying, "Good things are gonna happen to the entire company and especially to upper management. If this idea is implemented, it's gonna make all of us shine!"

2. Tie your idea to a corporate goal, mission, or vision. Quote verbatim all or sections of your corporate mission statement. All good companies have one. If yours does not, concoct one, for your company does have at least one goal—to sell

products and/or services (even if your outfit is producing low-quality products that no sane person would buy). Now you'll then have a far more receptive audience.

You really don't want to be perceived as "sucking up" to the senior execs, but for self-preservation, you definitely want to be seen not only as a team member but also a loyal supporter for the company's business philosophy. Sure enough, upper management will smile upon you for your benevolent dedication for the higher good of all!

3. Vow to "identify customer needs, develop innovative solutions, and deliver superior products and service excellence. Sounds like inspiring, action-oriented grist, doesn't it? But what does it actually mean? It doesn't matter one whit, as long as you pinpoint the connection between your idea and general sense of your company's direction and values. It's just a question of giving corporate values the right spin.

4. Emphasize that "our competitors are talking about this, so we've gotta beat 'em to the punch!" No one wants to assume responsibility for lagging behind the competition.

Get Right Timing

To this day historians declare that the Allies' Normandy Invasion of France in World War II was timely to the last detail. Those who study military strategy have written a number of books partly treating the fact that June 6, 1944, was *the only timely day* for D-Day. Either June 5 or June 7 might well have proved disastrous. If timing is everything, here is how to plan for precise timing:

As soon as you exclaim how marvelous the prospects will be *if your idea is accepted and implemented,* the wolves will smell blood. If your idea is amazingly brilliant, you run the gauntlet in risk of having it co-opted by the wolves—or at least the little foxes—before you've had the chance to firmly establish this as "my idea." Conversely, too, if the group feels your idea calls for refinement, the naysayers may shoot it down in a defenseless state.

It is ill-advised to publicize undeveloped ideas prematurely. This is not the time to drag out the soapbox. You're not selling a frontier elixir and moving from village to village. Besides, you don't relish putting up with the boo birds. Lie low in the early stages, quietly testing and polishing your idea. Then, as the concept is sharpened and shaped, attract the attention of your boss and other senior staffers. This bears repeating: *make ample use of testimonials or endorsements.* To gain support from others, cash in on the approval of the top brass.

Use Right Packaging

The culmination of your campaign will be your presentation to the management team. Adhering to marketing techniques, design your packaging as attractive as the product. So, employ *flim flam, gimmicks, bells,* and *whistles* adequately as follows:

Tailor the Presentation to the Audience

If the audience is junior, you can make a conceptual-cognitive-academic presentation. That'll impress 'em. *If you are addressing seniors,* keep your session simple. *Sesame Street* or *Rugrats* will decidedly suffice. Senior managers are burdened with "ships and sealing wax and cabbages and kings" (O. Henry)—in reality stock options and insider trading. You definitely don't want to bore them, and they bore easily, plus they have a short attention span!

If your content is weak, utilize an armada of graphs, charts, colors, and overlays. Follow the notes of the public speaker who wrote in the margin of his speech notes: "Weak point. Scream like hell and stomp!" In the good ole 1970s—when the humble flipchart was the major presentation aid—there was often an actual connection between the content of the chart and the content of the concept being presented.

Blessedly, with today's state-of-the-art, computer-generated presentations, we are not weighted down with this liability. Too many managerial types seem to think that multi-colored marks on contrasting backgrounds can have hypnotic, subliminal effects on our behavior. Far from encouraging dialogue, these presentations often garble solid communication (which is exactly what you desire if you have a weak argument!). If your would-be hearers are not buying into your spiel, overwhelm them with numbers. The numbers game! If you can't convince 'em, confuse 'em.

Keep it short. Without preamble, unveil your hottest idea immediately. Have you ever gone to a company picnic or other soiree, and then you had to wait two hours for what you attended for—**food**? The longer you drone on, the more liable your reluctant hearers are to disagree and even pan your concept. If you are speaking to senior management, limit your presentation to one or two points.

In the case of disagreement, sacrifice a chip or two you're willing to relinquish. If you concede a few suggestions from those critiquing your idea, they will conceive of you as flexible, pliable, and cooperative.

If your opponents continue to object, you take the high road. Never allow your pugnacious, hostile emotions to rear their grungy little heads (even if you feel your hearers are stupid, and maybe some of them are). Why condescend to their level? If you handle the situation adroitly, the bosses will recognize you as a veritable "statesperson," able to *rise above politics.* It is permissible to imply that nothing but gullibility can keep your hearers from the sickening effects of those who would dare to oppose your idea. Subtly mention that your opponents use arguments without substance. It will become obvious to the sophisticated decision-makers that your opponents lack moral fiber and that they don't practice what they preach.

Say It with the Right Tone

"You must remember this, a kiss is . . ." Good grief, you must remember this: how you say it is more pivotal than what you say. To your advantage, it is form and not substance that matters in any presentation. Don't deceive yourself and denigrate your presentation, even if you're trying to sell recycled toilet tissue! Your presentation should verify that you have the qualities of courage, pride, honor, honesty, dignity, integrity, duty, morality, decency, and values. If you do possess those, it probably rules out your becoming a politician! Frankly, this is how your profound ideas will tap into the imaginations of your hearers. They will absorb your honest, sincere, and well-crafted words . . . and approve your proposal!

Always employ acronyms. Wow, it sounds impressive when you ominously warn, "Our competitors may leapfrog us with their 'LRS.'" At the moment it doesn't matter that LRS has no meaning. If someone asks, have a meaning ready, like "Lateral Retention Systems" or "Low Retinal Symbiosis."

Use a deep, silky-smooth voice. If you're a woman, strive for Lauren Bacall, not Fran Drescher; a man, somewhere between Sam Donaldson and James Earl Jones, not Pee Wee Herman (Paul Rubens) and Woody Allen. Warm. Smooth. Rich. Enveloping. Practice it first. How not to do it? For several hours watch the book reviews on C-Span, a sure cure for insomnia.

With your honey-sweet voice, hypnotize them with: "My concept has at heart the best interests of our entire company. It will amplify our extraordinary mission statement." (This is especially pivotal if top management is present.) If you are praising others for their contribution, do it with a catch in your throat, with Mother-Teresa compassion. This will eloquently herald that you are people-oriented. That's a major component in your company's profile of a successful leader, but often it is mock compassion as they "downsize" another redundant employee.

Speak with conviction when you invoke your firm's value statement that "people are our greatest assets." But don't honestly add, "We have to get rid of a lot of our greatest assets." Once you've become adept at faking sincerity, you're winging it. You are then prepared to move from business to politics to La-La Land in show business.

Express gratitude and appreciation. When your concept is accepted, thank those who have bought into your brainstorm. In your brief thanks-giving speech, you might close out with: "As an immediate contribution to company cost-effectiveness, pledge to cut down on meetings, shorten presentations, and eliminate excessive audio-visuals. I encourage all of you to follow suit. Thank you. Thank you. Thank you. Muchas gracias!"

ACADEMIC SUMMARY

It is nigh onto impossible to overcome cognitive dissonance when persuading others to agree to, and then follow through, on anything, no matter how much or how little, even if it benefits the organization or others. If there is a disconnect between the idea and the receiver's self-image, so be it. Life is fleeting and transitory. One's career has only a limited number of self-promotion oppor-tunities in it.

So, make a concerted effort to reflect the nuance of language that connects with the variety of personalities and cultural norms reflected in the organization. These viable variations in meaning can have a telling impact. In fact, they may even impede the route to effective communications in lieu of succinct messages that are understood.

NOTE: If the academic summaries seem to make sense as you plumb further into this guide, you should become worried about it.

9. Dealing with Bureaucrats

Many of these bureaucrats have a full six pack but lack the plastic thing that holds it all together.
> —*Micro Daft Enterprises Executive*

Waging war on bureaucracy is the ultimate No-Bull Management challenge.
> —*Herb Gabora*

A bureaucrat's idea of cleaning up his files is to make a copy of every paper before he destroys it.
> —*General Hugh S. Johnson*

EXECUTIVE SUMMARY

The Corporate staff has the ill-defined role of managing the crucial appropriation of your company's resources. The actual, overriding assignment of these bureaucrats is to concoct various ploys with which to justify their existence.

These birds of prey can undercut your most strenuous efforts and drain your energy. Creative constructive avoidance described in this chapter is your most viable option. The tactics apply in dealing with all bureaucrats, whether corporate staffers, head office dweebs, or the government bureaucracies, with which you need to do business.

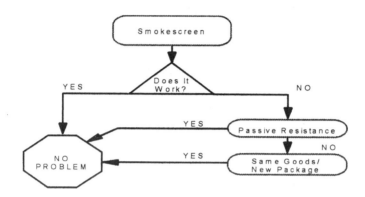

LEADER'S GUIDE

"You have a guest, Mr. Jabberwocky," Ms. Prudence Snidely, your receptionist, announces on the intercom. Being the affable, open-door person you are, you allow this unannounced "guest" to "walk right in, step right down." With a bright-toothed smile you greet this interloper until you hear those dreaded words: "Hello, I'm from Corporate. I'm here to help."

Dealing with bureaucrats is like taking a never-ending trip to the dentist for root canal procedures. Even if you are able to bypass the usual arrogance, sporadic crassness, intermittent insanity, chronic foolishness, notorious decisions,

They're here to help.

and memorable faux pas—not to mention the piles of reports you've completed in the past—these vultures are as unwelcome as the bubonic plague. A typical government bureaucrat takes pride in changing Dale Carnegie's *How to Win Friends and Influence People* to *How to Make Enemies and Distance People.* If you run into two persons talking, and one looks bored to tears, the head office staffer is the other one.

YOUR GOAL

Dealing with staff bureaucrats is tiresome, worrisome, and bothersome. Natch, your over-arching goal is to make these eavesdroppers disappear. This is tricky because, for the umpteenth time, management must scrutinize you from their mahogany and teakwood offices—via the prying eyes of snooping staffers. You must emanate an aura of cooperation and support. You see, staffers promulgate the career charts, across-company development assignments, succession plans, and high-potential lists. You can almost hear Elvis crooning, "Caught in a trap. Can't get out!"

SO HOW DO YOU DO IT?
Smokescreen

The ubiquitous Headquarters staffers are around to police whether policies and programs are "properly" interpreted and implemented by entities like yours. The more charts and graphs they can generate, tabulating wild deviations and trends, the more valuable they will become back at the Corporate office. It seems predetermined for

Corporate to strain its guts to uncover a division or unit that is non-compliant. If you and your cohorts are deemed uncooperative and not following the letter of Corporate law, the snoopers will show no mercy in instituting corrective measures. They will also guarantee that their punitive action is overly publicized. Justifying their actions is the key to their existence.

A Corporate "weenie's" stance is buttressed immensely if he or she is privy to esoteric, insider information. For the corporate KGB, access to information is a sure enhancement of perceived power. The head office staffer will always want to have a "rusty, trusty" mole inside each division to give grist to the most recent rumors and whispers. This sometimes elaborate spy network helps manufacture delusions of competence. No problem. Just use the following escape and evasion maneuvers.

☺ When you are pumped for info, offer only the bare-naked essentials, the rock-bottom minimum. Toss out tidbits that will launch the proverbial wild goose chase. If you are still being pressured for information, request—you guessed it!—clarification, and then additional clarification. Keep on talking amiably and energetically, deflecting the conversation to other topics. Likely the staffer will not realize that she/he has scraped the bottom of the barrel and has begun to excavate.

☺ If the staffer persists, suggest, "I'd appreciate additional instructions. Could you make this inquiry more specific? Thanks." Without being overtly obtuse, further request definitions of major terms and strategic content. "Oh, how does this align with the Company's vision and mission?" is a continuing diversion. This will more than likely ensure that this Corporate fink will be not so much of a has-been as an ultimate won't-be.

☺ It is exceedingly crucial that the Corporate staff glean multitudes of numbers. Simply give them the numbers they desire. So long as the numbers come out right, you have no worries about their paying attention to them. However, you must uncover what end result (the number) they want (or what they think they want). By all means, attach charts or graphs from an old survey or study to grant your numbers an air of authenticity. The Corporate staffer will leap for joy, even though what you have granted is meaningless.

Passive Resistance

The Corporate staff has a mandate to provide and promote coordination and leadership in company-wide initiatives. They relish this role, for it affords them ample scope to form standing committees, ad-hoc working committees, action groups, and task forces. They justify this on the basis of the necessity of synergy, coordination, inter-unit cooperation, information sharing, mutual problem-solving, and the need to invent new esoteric buzz words. This provides Corporate direction and, of course, job security.

You will probably be asked to serve on a task force or committee, which will likely meet and meet and meet . . . file a voluminous, padded report . . . and then do nothing about it. Step carefully. The following cryptic maneuvers are indispensable if you don't want your position questioned on the succession and promotion charts:

☺If you become involved, the time necessary for meetings, planning, research, agenda-setting, soliciting input, preparing minutes, and carrying out actions will keep you from doing *real work!* Graciously decline to serve. Not worth the aggravation. To boot, why jeopardize yourself by missing your numbers and falling out of the bonus plans at your division?

☺When you pass on their invitation to serve on a Corporate-designed make-work project, ex-press your keen interest in the idea and how you would simply adore the participation. "However, I'm so sorry I can't join the project now. There's a pressing situation that has suddenly arisen in our area." You can fill in the blanks with: "The reason is . . ."Labor negotiations. Budget cuts. Market crunch. Customer-service disaster, etc., etc., etc.

☺ Use your creativity. There are myriads of *pressing emergencies* from which to choose, even though you're not in the dry cleaning business. This dedicated diversion will cover your posterior but also maintain your reputation as an avid supporter.

Same Goods—New Package

You and I are aware that Corporate bureaucrats will carry out as many busy-work studies as they can get away with. All of them are designed to amass minutiae and to gauge the organization's current health. Naturally, surveys and studies make the troops as nervous as a long-tailed cat in a room full of rocking chairs. And interpretations of data can sometimes spew forth out-of-sight conclusions. They will literally drain you. Most often they will have no long-term impression beyond the initial "blood, sweat, and tears" (Sir Winston Churchill).

Heck, I bet you figured this out long ago. Many of Corporate's supposedly "new" studies are in reality archaic concepts with new buzzwords tacked on. Because the "new" programs are variations on old themes, you are beset with no real problems. This is all you have to do:

☺ Pull stuff from the shelf, from the files, or from the computers. Retool and repackage it with a new look . . . like that cleanser or detergent or toothpaste that is nearly always "new and improved"?

☺ If your refurbished "oldie" won't fit the Corporate guidelines, point out your unique situation. Explain that your organization's *distinctiveness* does not allow the information to be packaged and processed in the Corporate format.

☺ A goodly number of your colleagues will be hip to using these avoidance tactics. Thus, the Corporate weenies will be thrilled to find out anything. So, give them a small tidbit (e. g.: "Our costs are competitive."

Eventually the bureaucrats will fade away. More than likely the one who bugged you will fail to remember why you were contacted in the first place.

NOTE: If your boss suggests, "Cuthbert, I think it would be an excellent career move for you to accept a development transfer to Corporate," commence polishing up your resumé!

ACADEMIC SUMMARY

Muddify the fuzzification of Corporate-directed activity through the concurrent recognized objective of individual non-identification with perceived aberrant dysfunctional divergent goal-directed behavior from the perspective of the representatives from the senior structure within the Corporate configuration.

What the world really needs is another manual.

10. Honing Your Leadership Skills

There go my people. I must find out where they are going so I can lead them.
—*Alexander Ledra-Rollin*

The crowd will follow a leader who marches twenty paces ahead of them, but if he is thousand paces ahead of they will neither see nor follow him.
—George Brandes

His men would follow him anywhere, but only out of morbid curiosity.
—*Foster Brooks*

EXECUTIVE SUMMARY
Here is your roadmap to forging a reputation as a fireball, high-potential leader!

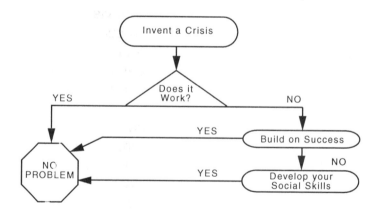

100

LEADER'S GUIDE

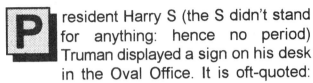resident Harry S (the S didn't stand for anything: hence no period) Truman displayed a sign on his desk in the Oval Office. It is oft-quoted: "The buck stops here." Leaders are defined most articulately by what they do. This chapter demonstrates how to capitalize on your exceptional leadership skills.

Your Personal Goal

Some people make things happen. Some people watch things happen. All too many people don't have the mistiest idea about what's happening. Stop in your tracks. Attention. As a leader your goal is for recognition as a leader who makes things happen, even if you are charisma-challenged and deficient.

So How Do You Do It?

I. Invent a Crisis

If you've seen the outlandish movie, *Wag the Dog,* you could probably skip this section. Concoct a bogus crisis. Why? To convince upper management that you must institute radical, far-sweeping changes and build a hefty budget to prop up your pet ideas.

The enemy could be the unions, your competitors, or any impending threat that might persuade the comptroller that the company is going "down the 'torlet,'" to quote Archie Bunker. Exaggerate any actual dilemmas, or whatever current scare, far out of proportions. Why again? To

Exaggerate the problem into a crisis.

obtain backing for approaches and actions your people would not accept under non-emergency situations. In a nutshell, this strategy is:

☺ *By hook or crook, you must convince management that the status quo is abominable.* Make a mountain out of the proverbial molehill. "It's sink or swim. This calls for immediate ER surgery all up and down the line. I can fix it if we'll follow through on these suggestions. Don't panic; let's move into action!"

Create an atmosphere of crisis so intense that the employees will go along with extreme actions and ideas that would, under pedestrian conditions, be unpalatable. For example: If you are responsible for Employee Relations, you could spin the isolated act of a single union supporter. All the union guy did was distribute a union circular in one facility. But you will pick up on that. "Why, that's a major union beachhead to organize and certify the entire company from coast to coast!"

☺ *Once senior management is spooked, whatever solution you recommend will be snapped up like raw meat suddenly made available to starving wolves.* Pretend you're Anthony Hopkins or Meryl Streep. Dramatically share this *watershed* breakthrough to all of the organization. Have the guts to announce, "This entire system is broken and desperate for repair. Major changes are in the offing." You Oscar Winner, you! You've designed the scenario for a landmark turnaround in the history of your firm. Your counterfeit crisis has evolved into a legendary Trojan Horse. This will open a gigantic gap for you to drive your pet agenda and your associated mammoth budget through.

Wowee! If this trumped-up-crisis ploy works,

the staff will rise up to call you "blessed," a *miracle worker* indeed. You will have etched yourself into your fellows' fond memories as a superb master leader who saved the day—and the company! Like the mythical Phoenix, your project will rise from the ashes. And you will accomplish it all without the Phoenix going through the fire or even being singed.

Yo, even if the original problem persists, all references to the crisis will have dissolved. (Just as Lee Iacocca was considered Chrysler's crisis-solving Savior . . . even though the basic problems still remained.)

II. Build on Success

The lead-pipe-cinch way to make yourself into the icon of an extraordinary leader is to crusade for winning causes, even if you have a minor role in implementing them. Nothing procreates success like success itself. Yet, success is in the eye of the beholder. Concentrate on this obsessive thought: All upper management remembers at bonus time are the Corporate slaves who are *meritorious* and those who are *unmeritorious*—in other words, the *bad guys*. Perhaps your boss may have a photographic memory when it comes to remembering you at bonus time, so he most probably will have the lens cover on. Your primary concern is for the shakers and movers to recognize you constantly as the person who has reached the summum bonum of leadership acumen.

Underline these three times in your little (color isn't important) book:

☺ *Your credibility will be amplified if you*

push and promote issues that are guaranteed winners (for instance, head a fundraising *drive for a charitable cause your boss' boss swears by)*. Oh, yeah, establish a task force, which is often disguised as teamwork or consensus-seeking. Bottom line: <u>This means no one is accountable!</u>

☺ *If this is a success, write an article (or have one of your confidants do one) for your company newsletter or bulletin or whatnot that turns the Klieg lights on you as the shining leader of this fantabulous victory.* You will further enhance the article if you supply the editor with candid photos of you in action. Keep those photo ops rolling. The hype machine can make you a marketable personality.

☺ *If the project begins to rot and stink, your front and back are protected since it's difficult to crack the whip with so many.* You can always alibi, "But all of the others agreed to it. OK?"

☺ *As the absolutely last resort, and if it's going down the water-closet pipes, accept the blame.* Bite the silver bullet. State in mellow, theatrical tones: "Yes, I made a mistake, but I remain confident that this experience will build bridges to our successful future." More than likely at least one good guy on the Management Team will suggest, "That's all right. Let's forget it. Why, anyone can make a mistake, as long as they learn valuable lessons from it." People are often forgiving . . . and your image as being sincere will be upgraded.

105

III. Develop Your Social Skills

Getting to know the right people socially will boost your rise up the Corporate ladder. Most of the crucial stuff in business is in reality hammered out on the golf course, on the racquetball or tennis courts, or in trendy restaurants. There you can hobnob with the right people. Believe it or not, if you cement "fruitful" social contacts, those connections will likely cut you some slack and give you rather good references, even if your work is sloppy and slovenly. You can't deny this maxim: you do get ahead on account of the people you know.

Your networking can make or break your career. Whatever you do, do it right and judiciously. Be cordial and attentive to those who can advance you in the company, but try not to slobber on them or fawn over them. Recognize that bosses are bosses and have the power of hiring and firing, but they are human beings as well who usually enjoy convivial company.

Try to avoid dead-air time during lunch or dinner meetings. When several are involved, sometimes you aren't able to cozy up to the exec who can do you the most good . . . but she'll/he'll remember you were there with the brain trust. Find out what interests the execs, whether it's sports, the theater, music, affairs, travel, whatever. You should become an expert at trivia. Bone up on *Jeopardy* and similar programs.

If you are a broken-down former jock, please don't tell old tales of your brilliant athletic feats, even though a few of them might be true. Since weather is often extreme these days, turn to that subject, which was also probably a favorite subject of the ancient cave dwellers. If the discussion should shift to work, watch your step. Reassure the brass that the company has superlative leadership. Gush forth with a pouring out of platitudes about "customer oriented, user friendly, and a spirit of winning." Your executives probably are painfully aware that the company is demoralized, disorganized, dysfunctional, and declining. Yet, they don't want to hear about the "four horsemen" of contemporary enterprises from you,

Business lunches also provide excellent networking opportunities. Just be sure to avoid the following potential problems: gaining the ill repute of being a freebie-addict who always orders the most expensive bottle of wine; making involuntary noises as you scarf down a 24-ounce steak in record time; and pretending to say "thank you" as you inebriatedly stagger from the restaurant with a huge doggy bag in hand.

ACADEMIC SUMMARY

Let us say, although it goes without saying, that, without being redundant, and since "brevity is the soul of wit" (Shakespeare), etc., etc., blah, blah—leaders need followers in order to be singled out as leaders, which means the followers need to believe the leaders do it!

11. Moving On

Big eight wheeler rollin' down the track,
Your true lovin' Daddy ain't comin' back,
He's movin' on, He's movin' on.
>   —*Hank Snow*

Try to see this experience in a positive
light.
>   —*Jack Kervorkian*

The biggest problem with experience is
that it often teaches you something you
don't want to know.
>   —*Guy Belleronti*

EXECUTIVE SUMMARY

If you are in trouble, buy time while you
are spiffing up your resumé and
networking with prospects and proph-
ets. The following chart can serve as a
roadmap to delaying and deferring the dreaded pink
slip until you are prepared to haggle for the optimum
possible severance:

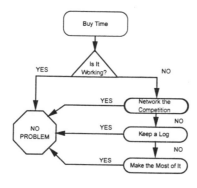

108

LEADER'S GUIDE

If you've been in the corporate world awhile, you're painfully aware that at times your firmament revolves. Once you were a shining star, but you have lost your Corporate twinkle. And your once royal jelly has turned into kiddy green slime. I hope not in your case, but sometimes your situation can become bad with a capital B (even if you have meticulously adhered to all of my sapient advice). If you're in trouble, ahem, it's probably your own fault. Maybe you were misreading and misinterpreting these chapters.

I don't even need to remind you what the signals are. I will anyhow. You're not being invited to strategic company confabs, you're not receiving pay raises or bonuses, and your business account and travel budgets have been diminished. If your boss keeps up his litany about *problems, problems, problems,* you're probably in trouble. I said *probably.* Some bosses are crabby even when all is copacetic. But the true indicator is . . . when your colleagues start to avoid you like you're "Typhoid Mary," you're toast.

YOUR PERSONAL GOAL

Come out a winner anyhow, come hell or high water!

So How Do You Do It?

Buy Time

It's worked before, and it can again. *Create diversions as you have done previously.* Allow yourself time to clean up your resumé and then send it all over. (When prettying up your occupational vita, take credit for any and all accomplishments of your group and your about-to-become-former boss.)

> We trained hard, but it seemed that every time we were beginning to form up into teams, we would be reorganized. I was to learn later that we tend to meet any new situation by reorganizing: and a wonderful method it can be for creating the illusion of progress, while producing confusion, inefficiency, and demoralization.

A highly workable diversionary scheme is to reorganize. This conjures up the illusion that positive stuff is in process. With this ploy you'll not only buy more time, but you'll craftily confuse people. The famed Roman philosopher, Petronius, wrote the above statement around 256 B.C.

If you master the strategies of ambiguity, procrastination, and the derring-do of zig-zagging and trapeze somersaulting, you will become the epitome of a miraculous survivor. Your mind-warping ability to suck and blow at the same time will go a long way toward convincing folks on opposite sides of any question that you are deep-down on their side. Keep on keeping on, as the expression goes, with your pirouettes and equivocations. Dither, waffle, baffle gab, and spend plenty of time out to lunch and breaks. Let your enemies put their arms around nothing but vapors.

If you are pounced upon to resolve an issue, try to get away by studying the problem, whether it is real or imaginary. The old time-killer of forming a task force, a working group, or an action committee is always nifty. (As you deem it advisable, add ad hoc to it.) Causing all the members of a study team to agree on anything at this stage is similar to rounding up stray sheep to sit for portraits.

It is imperative that at least one member of your study group be one level higher in the firm than you. Then, if what you're trying to achieve is a flat failure, that exec can be blamed for the abysmal flop. If at all possible, egg on this superior management type to make upbeat PR statements about your progress in spite of adversity, along with other impenetrable caveats and serpentine progressions.

Also purchase more time by studying other companies—your competition. You can sell this approach by suggesting that you must establish "benchmarks" or best practices from those successful companies in your industry. No thinking person could oppose striving to become a world-class organization. Of course, if you are allowed to select the companies, you will come up with those that have even more severe problems than your outfit.

Once again, if prodded for answers, reply that you are energetically pursuing several intriguing avenues. However, it is too early to speak about them. You are incubating a most creative solution. Only a little more time is necessary.

Network the Competition

How clever. Since you are studying industry's best practices, it may well give you the opportunity to meet some of your heftiest competitors. Follow up by carrying your counterparts from the competition to lunch. Through this you will discover other job options and have your reputation and resumé in circulation. Remember, by discussing your

Keep a log that contains exact quotes.

competitor's markets, products, and services, you can develop familiarity with the trade parlance. So, when you show up for an interview, you can employ the proper buzzwords and "in" terms.

Keep a Log

By all means keep copious notes, for at times situations can fall to pieces all too quickly. It will be essential that you have the correct information to cultivate your survival program. Write down the details of every encounter and meeting. This should contain exact quotes, so you can have the lowdown on all of the wackiness that goes on in the company. Collect photos from those weird rituals at the Corporate retreat—also pictures of clandestine liaisons consummated at the office Christmas party or at other occasions like picnics.

Having this embarrassing info on your boss and other upper managers can help immensely when you negotiate your personal severance package. (A tiny, easy-to-conceal tape recorder can certainly come in handy.) Why dive into a swimming pool devoid of agua?

Make the Most of It

In spite of all the sound counsel in these pages, unfortunately the worst can still occur. No problem! The feared pink slip doesn't have to be one of life's horrible traumas. Here you turn the lemon into lemonade. Your main chore is to focus your undivided attention on an excellent severance package.

Be happy. Don't worry. Don't give a second thought to what alibi you'll give your family and friends, that is, if you have any left. Whatever you hatch up probably won't ring true anyway. For example:

"I was overdue for a change." (Wishy-washy)

"I'll be happier." (You likely don't look happier.)

"I feel liberated, free as a bird." (Sounds flaky and "Free Bird" you ain't!)

"I have enough money to last for a while." (Sounds like you're involved in illegal activities.)

Regardless, this is still no time to call it fourth down and punt. Carry your cache of materials (namely, logs, tapes, pictures, and other incriminating evidence) to the termination meeting with your boss. Your boss will act as if he is more upset than you. No one but a miscreant—maybe the Marquis de Sade, Ivan the Terrible, and King Henry VIII, for instance—would relish firing people.

What a terrific time to transfer guilt to your boss! As your mother taught you, guilt is good. Use it to your best advantage. Recall all the incidents when your boss person disappointed you (only a week off when getting divorced; no time off when your neutered feline became severely pregnant). Recall all the occasions when she/he didn't support your magnificent ideas, like starting a hula-hoop revival and Charleston "jazzercise."

Pull a few of the juiciest tidbits from your briefcase—the log for starters. Then explain, "Boss, there is so much more here than you would care to talk about at this hurried session. I also can't confirm or deny that my lawyer has other corroborating evidence." Then trot out the pictures, play the tape, and bargain for all you're worth. A lot to you but not much to your about-to-be-ex-boss, but . . . he's becoming nervous as that cat on the hot tin roof. You can turn the worst into the best if you handle it adroitly.

A proper farewell from your company calls for dignity, panache, and amazing grace. You can parade out marching to your own drummer—and that's

No Bull!

ACADEMIC SUMMARY

Your challenge is to develop a personal continuous improvement process to reexamine and reflect upon your practices and to maximize your transitional redeployment opportunities. If cognitive dissonance continues, obfuscate incessantly, thereby delaying the dehiring process and enhancing your personal renewal and severance provisions. And when it's all over, consider your lessons learned . . . Coming right up!

12. Lessons Learned

That which gets recognized gets repeated.
—Kevin Jenkins of Canadian AirLines

You get what you are willing to accept.
—Author Unknown

Humor must have its background of seriousness. Without this contrast there comes none of that incongruity which is the mainspring of laughter.
—Max Beerbohm

Corporate turf wars can sometimes create a momentum all their own—sort of like the number of pages in this book that tell stories about the territorial games we play versus the small number of pages that describe how to take the bull out of management. Here are some fundamentals to success.

1. Humor Is Serious Business

Leaders deal with reality as they find it—not as they wish it to be. Politics have a dirty name in some quarters, but politics are a fact of life. You may as well get used to the situation. If you can discover humor in the foibles and frustrations of the modern workplace, you'll have more fun at work and in life. Current studies indicate a sense of humor is an important factor to be considered in the identification of high-potential employees. So why be considered low potential?

In the grand scheme of things, many of the goofy situations encountered at work deserve a smile, not ulcers. Laughter is a refreshing antidote to the serious *business of business.* If you laugh, then you can see the truth. As Sir Noel Coward once noted, "Work can be more fun than fun."

2. The Costs Are High When Game Playing Becomes a Way of Life

Politics will never go away. But some organizations lose a sense of balance. When office politics become pervasive and destructive, it becomes difficult to maintain a sense of humor. If work becomes a battlefield where employees, like soldiers, trudge to war daily and are hit by "friendly fire," the troops can become demoralized. Laughter and a cooperative spirit give way to negative attitudes and mentality of blame.

Vicious and cunning corporate territorial games are costly and non-productive. What is your perception of the costs to your organizational unit? (team, department, division, or company, whichever is smaller). Challenge yourself to this No-Bull University test.

Assess the bottom-line costs to your organization in terms of the loss of time, energy, synergy, and creativity consumed by organization politics. Use examples from this book and don't forget fudging data, "forgetting" tasks, discrediting others, droning on, sandbagging, stealing ideas, and good old-fashioned sucking up. You receive double bonus points if you can explain the role of your company's executives in all of this. Send your answer to your boss.

3. No-Bull Management Practices Impact the Bottom Line

Organization politics can be destructive or creatively managed. It's a question of leadership. Effective leaders know that the effort, time, and energy consumed in costly territorial games could be channeled into creating an environment that releases energy and inventive sparks. They don't waste everyone's time with management bull. They know managing is not complex. We have made a science out of making simple things complex. (Some management gurus have made a fortune out of this.)

Here is another No-Bull University test. Just answer this question, and you may qualify as a No-Bull Manager.

Assess the bottom-line impact in your organization, **If only** your execs *turned to instead of on* their employees when confronting a crisis; if everyone avoided misleading and deceiving employees and co-workers; engaged in direct and honest interpersonal communications; accepted personal responsibility for their actions; contributed to constructive teamwork; and respected the dignity of each individual.

4. Tone Makes the Difference

Some organizations have a positive, opportunity-oriented climate. Others have a stifling atmosphere. The tone in the former creates energy. The tone in the latter drains energy. Have you ever felt this difference in tone?

Have you noticed how the instinctive responses to a problem differ? In some organizations the natural impulse is to simply fix it. In other units, the probable reaction is to dump the problem on someone else, find fault, or blame others.

Some companies treat the customer as welcome; others treat customers as if they were a bloody nuisance.

118

No-Bull Management

In some departments, whining and complaining are the norm . . . in others, employees put their hearts into what they do. Some employees enjoy looking for better ways to do things; others will resist any and all changes. Some leaders pay attention to people; others pay attention to panaceas, quick fixes, "effortless" solutions, and buzz-words. And so it goes.

Effective leaders know that you can be results-oriented and have fun on the job. They know that the costs of dysfunctional organization politics are high. They foster common-sense practices that have a positive impact on the bottom line.

True leaders create a positive tone . . . then stay out of the way and let good th.ings happen.

Appendix
Challenges

Don't find fault; find a remedy.
> —*Henry Ford*

Don't just talk about it. Do it!
> —*Hannah Majers*

It's been an unbelievable effort . . . it's amazing what you can accomplish when no one cares who gets the credit.
> —*Philip Fulmer, Head Coach of the 1998 NCAA Football Champions, The Tennessee Volunteers*

A PERSONAL CHALLENGE

This is a challenge to you and your organization to have fun and make money. Bull appears in many shapes and in many places. It will require the combined efforts of us all to transform our organizations into places of quality and effectiveness. Make a daily habit to eliminate behaviors and practices that will inhibit human performances. Let the cream rise to the top.

Manage by results, not appearances, politics, or fear. Inject humor and inspiration. You will get a lot more done and have fun doing it! **NO BULL!**

Final Exam

After considerable consultation with Mensa and the Albert Einstein Clone Club, this assiduously prepared examination is designed to test your understanding of your competency as a **No-Bull Manager.**

Organization Theory:

Describe the Corporate form of organization structure from its origin to the present day, concentrating especially, but not exclusively, on its social, political, economic, and philosophical impact on organization politics. Be brief, concise, and specific.

Communications:

Two thousand five hundred riot-crazed British soccer fans are storming your cafeteria. Calm them. You may employ any ancient language except Latin or Greek. Your intervention must be politically correct.

Re-engineering:

Create a customer service excellence for the government. The required performance standard is that all public service employees treat citizens as customers and provide courteous, friendly, and efficient service all of the time.

Entrepeneurialism and Creativity:

Write a piano concerto. Perform it with flute and drum. Orchestrate for a symphony and sell your opus to the New York Philharmonic for $100,000.

People Management:

Based on your knowledge of their work, evaluate the emotional stability, degree of adjustment, and No-Bull Management capability of each of the following: Alexander of Aphrodisias; Ramses II; Gregory of Nicea; and Hammurabi. Support your evaluation with quotations from each leader's writings.

Strategic Planning:

What would you do if independent counsel Ken Starr had a mandate to investigate your indiscretions? Review your plan with your significant other before submitting to your local newspaper.

Teamwork:

Estimate the problems in group dynamics within your company which might accompany a Stock Market crash. Construct an experiment to test your theory.

Management Science:

Define management. Define science. How do they relate? Why?

Propound a generalized algorithm to optimize all managerial decisions.

Leadership:

The disassembled parts of a high-powered rifle have been placed on your desk. You will also locate an instruction manual, printed in Hindi. In ten minutes a hungry Bengal tiger will be admitted into your office. Take whatever actions you feel appropriate. Be prepared to justify your decision.

International Business:

There is a red telephone on the desk beside you. Start a Trade War. Report at length on the socio-political and economic effects, if any.

Business Ethics:

Take a position for or against truth. Prove the validity of your position. (Lawyers are exempt from answering this question.)

Management Information Systems:

Explain the nature of information. Include in your answer an evaluation of the impact of the development of mathematics on software systems. Prove your thesis.

Management Theory:

Describe in detail. Be objective and specific.

Statement of Truthfulness . . .

I_____ on this day, _____
(Leave out the year. Who knows what'll happen with the Y2K millennium dilemma?), have successfully completed this examination with no help from my friends or my enemies. (Note: It is best to take the examination in a private room while you are in the altogether, having nothing before you but the test and two writing instruments. You are forbidden to have the answers tattooed on your skin. Before you enter the cubicle, a cer-tified nurse will inspect your body cavities to ascertain whether you have hidden the answers.)

Certification

If you pass the final exam, you will be eligible for certification from No-Bull University. This also en-entitles you to wear the graduate's jacket.

No-Bull University

setting the standards in lower learning

In recognition of efforts in removing barriers to human & organizational accomplishment

Hon. Harold McAlindon, Esq.

**is awarded the honorary degree of
Doctor of No-Bull Management (Nb.D.)**

Toros Bullicus Extrementius in Organizatiale

January 12, 1999

Date

Herb Gabora, **President**

Signed

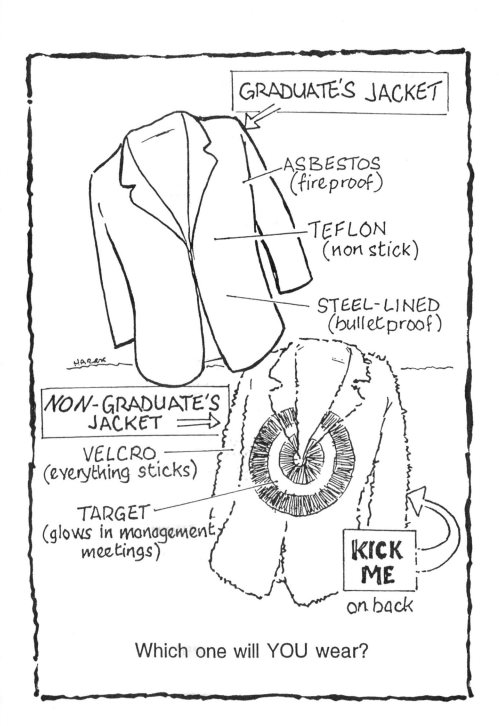

GRADUATE'S JACKET

ASBESTOS (fireproof)

TEFLON (non stick)

STEEL-LINED (bulletproof)

NON-GRADUATE'S JACKET ⇒

VELCRO (everything sticks)

TARGET (glows in management meetings)

KICK ME on back

Which one will YOU wear?

This presentation is based on the book "No Bull Management". To obtain a copy (including all the graphics used in this presentation), contact the author, Herb Gabora.

Presenter Biography

Herb Gabora

President, Organization Advantage
1005 Flintlock Ct, Nashville TN
615-399-7805
fax: 615-361-3982
hgabora@bellsouth.net

Herb Gabora is a registered Organization Development Consultant and has been involved in major organization change and team effectiveness projects over the last twenty-five years. He has consulted with a range of companies including Spar Aerospace, Bayer Inc., Milgo Solutions, and the Economic Development Corp. Herb has had previous executive experience with Mitel Corporation, Nortel Networks, and Bell-Northern Research. Herb has taught at several universities and has made conference presentations in the U.S., Canada, Japan and Ireland. He is the author of the business satire, No-Bull Management, and has published numerous articles on management and organization issues.